The Cambridge Manuals of Science and
Literature

T0352029

THE WANDERINGS OF PEOPLES

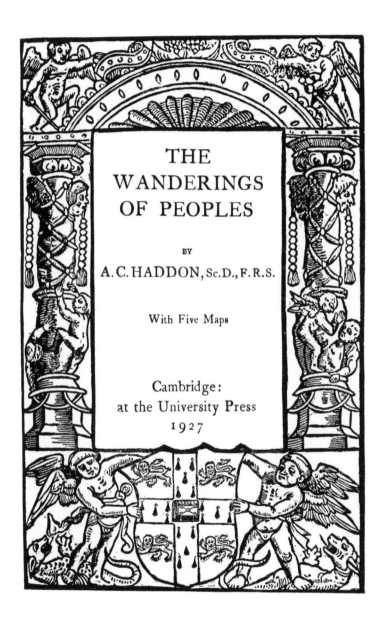

THE WANDERINGS OF PEOPLES

BY

A. C. HADDON, Sc.D., F.R.S.

With Five Maps

Cambridge:
at the University Press
1927

CAMBRIDGE UNIVERSITY PRESS
Cambridge, New York, Melbourne, Madrid, Cape Town,
Singapore, São Paulo, Delhi, Mexico City

Cambridge University Press
The Edinburgh Building, Cambridge CB2 8RU, UK

Published in the United States of America by
Cambridge University Press, New York

www.cambridge.org
Information on this title: www.cambridge.org/9781107605862

© Cambridge University Press 1927

This publication is in copyright. Subject to statutory exception
and to the provisions of relevant collective licensing agreements,
no reproduction of any part may take place without the written
permission of Cambridge University Press.

First Edition, 1911
Reprinted (with corrections) 1912, 1919, 1927
First paperback edition 2012

A catalogue record for this publication is available from the British Library

ISBN 978-1-107-60586-2 Paperback
Additional resources for this publication at www.cambridge.org/9781107605862

Cambridge University Press has no responsibility for the persistence or
accuracy of URLs for external or third-party internet websites referred to in
this publication, and does not guarantee that any content on such websites is,
or will remain, accurate or appropriate.

With the exception of the coat of arms at
the foot, the design on the title page is a
reproduction of one used by the earliest known
Cambridge printer, John Siberch, 1521

PREFACE

My object in writing this little book is to give a brief survey of the trend of human migrations so far as our imperfect knowledge permits, and I have endeavoured to do this for various periods of human history, even going as far back as the earliest diffusions that can be predicated. It has not been easy to compress into so small a space the account of the various migrations, indeed little more could be done than merely indicate without describing the movements, their causes and effects. Much interesting information has thus had to be whittled down to a bare statement. I have introduced dates when possible, but in many cases these are only approximate, and it sometimes happens, as in Egyptian chronology, that the system of dating of one authority differs widely from that of another. This is the first time, I believe, that this task has been attempted, and consequently many errors may have crept in. The study of human migrations emphasises the fact that ethnology and history can be satisfactorily elucidated only from the geographical standpoint.

The bibliographies do not profess to be exhaustive, but a sufficient number of references have been given to enable the reader to check most of the statements made.   The numbers in thick type refer to authors mentioned at the end of each section, those of the pages being printed in light type.

It has been thought desirable to provide the reader with maps showing the more important migrations. Owing to the small size of the page these movements could be only approximately represented as regards direction, and chronology has had to be entirely left out of account, except in so far as prehistoric migrations in some instances have been indicated by dotted lines.   A number of historic movements, particularly in the case of Folk-wanderings of central Europe, have had to be omitted for the sake of clearness.

In conclusion, my thanks are due to Mr E. C. Quiggin, and especially to Mr H. M. Chadwick, for their advice in respect to the section on Europe, and I must also acknowledge the great assistance which I have received from Miss Lilian Whitehouse in the compilation of this book, and in the construction of the maps.

A. C. HADDON

24th May 1911.

CONTENTS

THE WANDERINGS OF PEOPLES

CHAPTER I

INTRODUCTION

THE movements of peoples are determined by two main factors, which may be briefly described as the driving force and the control; or, in other words, the cause of a migration is due to one set of circumstances and its direction to another.

When reduced to its simplest terms a migration is caused by an expulsion and an attraction, the former nearly always resulting from dearth of food or from over-population, which practically comes to the same thing. Sooner or later, a time comes when the increase of the population of a country exceeds its normal food-supply. Among hunting communities the game may be so reduced by over-hunting or by disease that it cannot support even a stationary or decreasing population. The chief danger to be feared by pastoral peoples is lack of water; a succession of small droughts can make pasturing unprofitable, but when a whole

A   1 country definitely becomes more arid, migrations on a large scale are inevitable. Evidence has now accumulated which proves that various regions of the earth have undergone slow climatic changes, and that a given area at one period of time may be more or less wooded, while at another, owing to a drier climate, steppes arise, or even desert conditions may supervene. Changes of this nature occurred in parts of Europe during the ages when Palæolithic men hunted reindeer and chased bison and wild horses; and the desiccation of central Asia has had a profound effect upon human history in Europe as well as in Asia. Agriculturists are affected in the same way; but to a certain extent, by means of irrigation in some cases, and by more intensive cultivation in others, the soil may be made to support an increased population; nevertheless, a limit is soon reached, unless the resources are supplemented by trade.

It is probable that a migration induced by an attraction is rare as compared with that produced by an expulsion, for as a rule people are loth to leave their fatherland, and it usually requires the double set of circumstances to uproot them.

The simplest cases of migration by attraction are those of a people living on poor steppes or plateaus adjoining cultivated land or rich valleys. Agricultural peoples are, as a rule, averse to and ill-prepared for war, and the more prosperous their circumstances, the more they are likely to be enervated by their very civilisation. They are thus liable at all times to be attacked by neighbouring brigands, who in some cases retire to their barren homes with their booty, but in others remain among the conquered people, and, assimilating with them, in due course become more civilised, and in their turn are subject to invasions from their barbarian kinsmen of the borders. Thus is set up an automatic social mechanism which at the same time civilises the barbarians and energises those who have become softened by easy circumstances. To take but two examples : the walled towns of Ancient Greece in the centre of valleys opening out to the sea point to a danger from the brigands of the mountains, and possibly also from pirates from the sea ; and the inhabitants of the rich plains of Assam from time immemorial have been subject to raids and settlements by the hill tribes. When people become agglomerated in towns, especially where they have gained notoriety for their riches, the temptation for looting becomes very strong, but as a rule such enterprises do not lead to a permanent migration.

Hunger and loot are not the only impulses towards migration. The restless disposition of the " winners of the west " of North America was not due to an inability to maintain an existence in the Eastern

States, nor to an expectation of speedy riches. A craving for land—for more and more land—is only a partial explanation; sentiment, and a reaction against even the slightest of social restraints, had a great deal to do with it. Gold rushes are different, as wealth may thus be speedily gained by rapid exploitation.

Freedom from social, political or religious bondage has resulted in migrations of various kinds, like the exodus of the Hebrew bondmen from Egypt, the voyage of the *Mayflower*, or the trekking of the Boers. Religious enthusiasm may stimulate race expansion and lead to shiftings of population, as is seen in the histories of Buddhism, Islam, and Christianity. The partnerships of the crescent and the sword, of the cross and the gold of El Dorado, have been based upon a double enthusiasm.

The movements of peoples which are sufficiently dramatic for the ordinary historian to record, are often of less importance than the quiet, steady drift of a population from one area into another, as, for example, in the emigration from Europe to America in modern times. Movements of this kind may result in a noticeable or even a fatal depletion of a country, and the parent country may long remain desolate, or may be filled up in course of time by an alien people, as in the case of eastern Germany and the Slavs (p. 47). Although immigrant peoples may bring a culture and language permanently affecting the conquered peoples, yet the aboriginal population, if allowed to survive in sufficient numbers, will eventually impair the racial purity of the new comers, and there is a tendency for the indigenous racial type to reassert itself and become predominant once more.

The control of a migration is due mainly to geographical conditions. Movements of men, like those of fluids, take the line of least resistance, flowing, as it were, in channels or open areas bounded by barriers. The latter are of variable resistance ; thus, if an open area or a valley is densely populated it may offer a greater resistance than a geographical barrier, and the tide of migration would then flow over or along the barrier. Barriers are thus relative, and only in rare cases are they insurmountable.

An open country is most liable to early occupation, as the labour of felling trees with stone implements is very great ; even with iron axes there is considerable difficulty in clearing a forest, a difficulty which becomes enormously increased in tropical jungles. For the same reason an open country is subject to frequent invasions. River valleys, for various reasons, early supported relatively large populations, but the rivers themselves, as a rule, afforded an easy means for ingress to seafaring invaders. Steppes present great difficulties to

agriculturists, unless they are supplied with
mechanical means for breaking up the soil and reap-
ing the harvest ; on the other hand, steppes form the
natural home for pastoral peoples, who by their
mobility are usually able to keep off intruders. When
a hunting population occupies an open country or
a steppe, it is ultimately replaced by a pastoral
people, especially if the invaders be also tillers of
the soil, for the more they are prone to agriculture
the more complete is their usurpation of the land.
A pastoral or semi-pastoral people, however, can
only migrate along a country which affords sufficient
pasturage and watering for their flocks ; mountains,
forests, deserts, swamps, and the sea form obstacles
which are practically insuperable for such peoples.
In Africa, at all events, a further barrier towards
migration may be found in the tsetse fly, ticks, and
other insect pests, which afford intermediate hosts
for the parasites of various kinds of cattle diseases.

Mountain chains are obvious barriers which deflect all movements on a large scale, but usually
they can be pierced across the passes by the strenuous
efforts of armed bands. Even the Romans did not
attack the Germans till they had secured their
position in Gaul and could find an easy entrance into
central Europe. On the other hand the slopes or
plateaus of a mountain chain may serve as a bridge
when the surrounding country is difficult to traverse.

The movements of peoples may not result entirely from causes which appear to be immediate, but are traceable in some instances to a remote event having at first sight no connection with them. Even an artificial barrier, as Ujfalvy suggests, may have far-reaching effects: " The building of the great wall of China was an event fraught with the greatest consequences, and one may say without exaggeration, that it contributed powerfully to the premature downfall of the Roman Empire " (**1**, 24).

Another type of artificial barrier is produced by the dominance of neighbouring countries by a powerful empire, which prevents the encroachment of barbarian peoples into countries thus protected. Examples of this are seen in the great empires of the East, the Egyptian dominance of Syria, and the Roman Empire. When the central government became weak, the way was again open for invasion.

The possession of more deadly weapons, improved implements for daily needs, or better means of transport, such as horses or camels, vehicles, or seaworthy vessels, has given their owners a decisive superiority on coming in contact with worse equipped peoples. These advantages have been potent factors in producing changes of population.

Not only is it necessary fully to comprehend existing climatic conditions and geographical features in order to understand human migrations, but it is equally necessary to reconstruct the conditions of different periods since the appearance of man. This is essentially the work of geologists, geographers, and meteorologists. The data are very scanty, and until more have been accumulated and the conditions reconstructed, ethnologists will be unable to elucidate the early history of man.

Our knowledge of the movements of peoples in various parts of the world during the historic period, that is, since the time when man learnt to write his records, is meagre, even in regard to civilised areas; elsewhere, and for prehistoric periods, recourse must be had to tradition and archæological evidence. Both these sources of information have to be utilised with extreme caution, but where they agree a fair degree of probability if not of certainty can be attained.

The evidences for migrations are to be sought mainly in the physical characters of peoples, their artifacts, customs, folk-tales, and language.

The physical characters of an isolated people are usually fairly obvious, though their accurate description is difficult, and becomes still more so when racial mixture has taken place. The effects of hybridisation are as yet very imperfectly understood, as are the effects of change of environment; the disentanglement of racial elements in a mixed people, therefore, requires the greatest care.

Artifacts, that is objects made by man, are often brought forward as evidence of racial movements, but their occurrence may be due merely to borrowing. Archæology bears the same relation to technology that palæontology does to zoology, and the objects with which it deals are fossils in the true sense of the term. The evidence of either must be treated in a similar manner. For example, ethnologists learn how to recognise the artifacts of a given people and the differences between them and similar objects made by other peoples ; frequently characteristics of material, form, technique, or decoration, are so marked that many objects can be definitely assigned to a particular group of people or to a limited area. In process of time form, technique, and decoration may become modified, and then it is necessary to determine whether this indicates that definite evolution has taken place *in situ*, or whether influences have come in from elsewhere. If the latter can be proved, the question arises whether the change is due to the immigration of another people into the district, that is a " racial drift " ; or whether the innovations are the result of the imitation of objects that have arrived by means of loot or trade, that is a " cultural drift," for there can be little doubt that import trade if considerable and pro-tracted will exert a marked influence on native

manufactures. The introduction and methods of
utilisation of domestic animals and plants may be
considered as analogous to the foregoing. For
instance, the introduction of the horse into America
was due to a racial drift, but its employment by
the Plains Indians and by the Indians of the Pampas
of South America was a cultural drift.

The same argument applies to a certain extent
to customs, and religious ideas and ceremonies.
In the latter cases there is probably always some
personal influence, but the results may be dis-
proportionate to the numbers ; in these instances
the racial drift may be inappreciable, or may not
affect the local population in the least, while the
cultural drift may be quite noticeable.

There has been great discussion concerning the
evidential value of folk-tales with regard to cultural
drift and racial drift.   There is no doubt that
they can be passed on from one people to another,
but owing to the essential uniformity of human
thought the same simple motives can originate
independently. When complex tales occur, however, in different countries, then there is a *prima
facie* case for borrowing.   Further, folk-tales,
especially those dealing with mythology, often re-
flect earlier conditions in a different geographical
environment.

It is astonishing with what ease a people can

adopt a foreign language, which, however, almost invariably undergoes structural and phonetic modification in the process. For example, the great groups of Indo-Germanic languages mainly result from subject peoples having adopted the speech of their alien conquerors. The earlier language of a country, which in some cases underwent sound-shiftings, for instance, the Germanic languages (**2**, 330), often survives in place-names. Language is a criterion for racial-contact but not necessarily for migration. On the other hand, language has proved of great assistance in determining the affinities and the movements of peoples in the New World.

1. UJFALVY, C. DE. *Les Aryens au nord et au sud de l'Hindou-Kouch*, 1896.

2. FEIST, S. *Beitr. z. Gesch. d. deutschen Sprache u. Lit.*, xxxvi., 1910.

PETRIE, W. N. FLINDERS. *The Revolutions of Civilisation*, 1911. (*Cf.* especially chapters vi. and vii.)

MYRES, J. L. *The Dawn of History*, 1911.
(These suggestive little books have appeared since the above was in print.)

KEANE, A. H. *Man Past and Present*. New edition by A. Hingston Quiggin and A. C. Haddow. Cambridge, 1919.

CHAPTER II

Two high plateaus occupy nearly two-fifths of the area of Asia. One, that of western Asia, includes Anatolia, Armenia, and Iran (Persia, Afghanistan, and Baluchistan), the other, the lofty plateau of central Asia, stretches from the Himalayas to the north-east. These vast regions, mostly unfit for agriculture or even for human settlement, assume the character of poor steppes and deserts, and divide Asia into two parts : 1, the lowlands of Siberia and the Aral-Caspian basin, and 2, the lowlands of Mesopotamia, India, China, and Manchuria.

The great central plateau consists of several broad terraces, contains mountain-ranges, and is fringed by lofty border-ranges, which along the north-west border are cut into by wide trenches that lead by easy gradients down from the plateau to the lowlands. The most important of these is the " Jungarian Gate," and it was down this gently sloping trench that the Mongol inhabitants of the plateau went west to invade the Ural region and Europe.

12

Fringing this plateau, from the Tian-shan to the Verkhoyansk Mountains, is a broad Alpine zone, the terraces of which are covered with a luxuriant grass vegetation, affording good pasturage, while the slopes of the hills are wooded and form rich hunting grounds, but not even the valleys are suitable for agriculture. Beyond this is an extensive, lofty, undulating plain, which varies from a dry steppe through pastoral land to the rich wheat lands of south-west Siberia. A similar belt of elevated plain runs round the south-east edge of the great plateau, and those parts of the plain which are covered with loess are the abode of a dense agricultural population.

The lowlands proper, which extend over the rest of Siberia, consist in the south of marshy forests unsuitable for settlement, and further north of treeless, barren, and even frozen tundra. East of the loess in China is the great alluvial plain of the north, but to the south is a forested mountain area, which stretches to the confines of India; the larger valleys open out into fertile alluvial plains, in which civilisations have sprung up. Similarly the valleys of the Ganges and Indus have long been centres of civilisation, while the jungle-covered highlands of southern India still harbour tribes of uncivilised hunters. Mesopotamia, or the broad valley of the Tigris and Euphrates, was the cradle of civilisation in the remotest antiquity (Kropotkin, **1**, 345).

When at its greatest expansion during the last phase of the Glacial age, the ice covered nearly the whole of Eur-Asia to the north of the 50th parallel (with the exception of the lowlands of Siberia, which represented gulfs in the Arctic Ocean) and a very large portion of the highlands to the south of this line. As the ice thawed immense lakes were formed, which in the process of desiccation became extensive marshes studded with countless smaller lakes ; later these became prairies, and later still in some cases arid deserts. Thus there has been a gradual desiccation of the greater part of Asia and Europe since Glacial times (Kropotkin, **1**, 722) ; but as Huntington has shown (**2**) this secular desiccation has been varied by fluctuations, indeed Brückner suggests that in about every thirty-six years the whole world passes through a climatic cycle. Another series of climatic changes comprises the fluctuations which took place simultaneously over the northern hemisphere during the Glacial epoch, and there appears to have been an analogous and intermediate series of pulsations during the historical period in central Asia. The periods of deficient rainfall in the Brückner cycles during the nineteenth century were marked in various parts of the world by rebellions, wars, and shiftings of populations (**2**, 373). If these minor fluctuations had such important effects on history, the greater climatic changes must have had a tremendous influence on the conditions affecting the life of mankind.

It may reasonably be held that man evolved somewhere in southern Asia, possibly during Pliocene or Miocene times, and it is not unreasonable to suppose that the early groups were not unlike one another, but possessed a tendency to variability which would be directed to some extent by geographical conditions and fixed by isolation. As Palæolithic man was certainly inter-glacial in Europe we may assume that man was pre-glacial in Asia. The incoming of the Glacial period would start movements, which would be alternately relaxed and accentuated during the inter-glacial mild periods and those of increased cold ; during the former the movements would probably be those of simple expansion, but during the latter of propulsion. Assuming the relative, but not the absolute, heights of the Asiatic plateaus in late or post-Pliocene times to have been similar to what they are at present, it may be suggested that a narrow-headed human variety occupied the lower lands to the north of the plateaus, eventually spreading to America. As there was more than one race of man in Europe in Palæolithic times, there were probably several narrow-headed (dolichocephalic) varieties in Asia, which may have differentiated by Neolithic times into distinct races; some of these may have become mixed with broad-headed (brachycephalic) peoples and thus formed several of those obscure west Asiatic peoples whose affinities it is so difficult to unravel. The tall, fair, blue-eyed dolichocephals of north Europe are generally believed to be a variety of the Mediterranean race, but these may equally well be two varieties of a common stock, the former probably having their area of characterisation in the steppes north of the plateaus of Eur-Asia, and migrating eastwards and westwards as the country dried after the last glacial phase. It will be convenient to speak of them as Proto-Nordics. The prehistoric dolicho-cephals (Chudes) of southern Trans-Baikalia (3, 270), the builders of the tumuli (kurgans) of southern Siberia, and the dolichocephalic kurgan-builders of south Russia, probably belonged to this stock which later appears to be represented by the blond, blue-eyed Usuns or Wu-suns (who lived on the northern slopes of the Tian-shan in Chinese Turke-stan, and gave so much trouble to the Chinese two hundred years B.C.), and also by the Sacæ (and their modern descendants the Balti), the western Scythians, and the Nordics of north Europe. These were mobile peoples who preferred a pastoral to an agricultural life and therefore were a source of unrest to their neighbours. While Mongoloid peoples may have existed around the central plateaus, the true Mongol type appears to have differentiated on those table-lands, whence in times of stress they poured forth on the neighbouring lowlands. The western plateaus were the area of characterisation of another brachycephalic race, which includes short and tall varieties, but is not at all "Mongolian." This Alpine race (**17,** 208) extends from the Hindu Kush to Brittany; here and there descents have been made into the lowlands, but it remains an essentially upland people. Western Asia is the home of two main brachycephalic peoples, the Turki and Ugrians, who were doubtless of more or less common origin; usually they are stated to be a very early cross between Proto-Nordics and Alpines, with, in places, occasional Mongol mixture. On the other hand they may be descendants of an intermediate variety between the two former types. South of the plateaus brunet dolichocephals wandered west and east; traces of this stock are found scattered in south-east Asia, for example the Man-tse of south China, and it is the essential element in the Indonesians and possibly also in the Dravidians of India. Some of the last are mixed with a much lower race, the Pre-Dravidians, survivors of whom may be

B

found among certain jungle tribes, *e.g.* the Veddas of Ceylon and the Sakai of Malacca. The last remnants of a Negroid stock are the pygmy Andamanese and the Semang of Malacca.

The general trend of the heterogeneous populations of northern Asia has been from south to north, not on account of any attraction, but as a result of pressure. Thus the Chukchi drove other tribes before them, as they were themselves driven north by Tungus and others, though when their strength had been greatly increased by the introduction of reindeer-breeding they were able to repel the Tungus. The Yakut, representatives of the old Turki stock, perhaps themselves driven north by the Buryat (who at the time of the first Mongol invasion in the thirteenth century moved from Amur into the Baikal region), thrust themselves between the Tungus tribes to the mouth of the Lena, and introduced cattle-breeding on the pastures of the Lena (**13**, 209 ff.)

The cradle of the Turki appears to have been the Altai ; migrations have from early times flowed south-westwards from this area, one of which ultimately landed the Osmanli in Europe in the middle of the fourteenth century A.D. (p. 47). The Finno-Ugrian stock, physically allied to the Turki, but linguistically distinct (**15**, 21) originated in close proximity, about the headwaters of the Yenisei.

The Samoyed branch drifted northwards to the Arctic Ocean and are said to be still migrating westwards, a small group having recently settled in Russian Lapland (4). The Finnish branch followed the course of the Irtish to the Urals, which formed a second centre of dispersion, which Szinnyei (15) suggests was their original home. Thence movements took place down the Pechora and Dvina to the Arctic seaboard. Others followed the Kama to the Volga, where permanent settlements were formed ; detachments from these spread south and west as far as the Danube by the seventh century A.D. (p. 45). Meanwhile, the true Finns wandered up the Volga and into what is now Finland (3, 333) ; but cf. Ripley (22, p. 358).

The earliest known civilisation in the world arose north of the Persian Gulf among the Sumerians, a people speaking an agglutinative language, who are regarded by some as being of Ural-Altaic (Turki or Ugrian) stock. But the Babylonians of history were a mixed people, for Semitic influence, according to Winckler (20, 2), began to flow up the Euphrates valley from Arabia during the fourth millennium B.C. This influence was more strongly felt, however, in Akkad than in Sumer, and it was in the north that the first Semitic empire, that of Sargon the Elder (c. 2500 B.C. according to E. Meyer), had its seat. The Assyrians were still further semitised by a second migration, termed Canaanitic or Amoritic,

several hundred years later. The supremacy of
Babylon was first established by the dynasty of
Hammurabi (c. 1950 B.C., earlier according to
Winckler), which was overthrown by the Hittites
about 1760 B.C. (**16**). Then followed the Kassite
domination, which lasted from about 1760 to 1100
(**19,** 425). The Kassites, who appear to be identical
with the Cossæi of later times, a people settled
between Babylon and Media, are of unknown
origin. They were the foremost tribe of a great
movement of peoples occasioned by the arrival or
expansion of the " Aryans " in Bactria and eastern
Iran between 2300 and 2000 B.C.,[1] who perhaps
brought Ural-Altaic tribes with them. The Kassites
overran Media and Elam, whence they spread across
the Tigris to Babylonia. It was probably due to
them that the horse, first introduced by the
" Aryans," became common in south-west Asia (**5**);
it was introduced into Babylon about 1900, but
was unknown in Hammurabi's reign. They were
gradually absorbed by the ancient civilisation, and
Semitic influence reasserted itself once more in the
third migration from Arabia, the so-called Aramæan,
believed by Winckler to have taken place from the

---

[1] E. Meyer (*Z. f. vgl. Sprachwiss.*, xlii. p. 16) believes that the
" Aryans " remained in the region east of the Aral and Caspian until
about 2000 B.C., and after that time began to make their way eastwards into India and south-westwards.

middle of the second to the first half of the first millennium (20, 3, 7 ; 6, 15.) Associated with the Kassites were Aryan-speaking bands similar to those who conquered Mitani (in the westward bend of the upper Euphrates) by about 1500 B.C.

The southward movement of the " Aryans " into Bactria was fateful in history, for it cut off the jade and other trade between Kotan and west Asia; the " Aryan " conquest of Mitani separated Babylonia from Syria, thus deflecting trade to the Red Sea route. These Mitani chiefs preserved traces of a stage of culture somewhat, but not much, earlier than that indicated in the *Rig Veda*. An eastern branch of the " Aryans," perhaps also associated with Turki tribes, moved eastward and took possession of the pasture lands of the western Panjab about 1700 B.C. (5, 1119). In later times the " Aryans " of Mitani were called by the Greeks Mattienoi ; they are possibly the ancestors of the modern Kurds. The mountaineers of Elam on the east continually debouched on to the rich plains of Mesopotamia, and *c.* 1180 B.C. Babylon was wasted by a second Elamite invasion.

From early historical times Syria was inhabited by Semitic peoples. Further groups of Semitic stock constantly invaded the land from the south, partly because of its intrinsic value, and partly because it occupied the strategic position with regard to the trade between Asia, Egypt, and Europe, and afforded opportunities of plundering the wealthy cities on these trade routes. Changes of climate or movements of peoples may also have contributed to drive them from their own home. The earlier invasions may have coincided with the first expansion into Mesopotamia during the fourth millennium B.O. A second wave of Semitic migration spread from Arabia northwards and westwards (Winckler's Canaanitic or Amoritic Migration, 20, 3). These Semitic movements may have had some bearing upon the supposed migration of the Phœnicians from the Persian Gulf to the Syrian coast, where they had established themselves by about 2000 B.O., for the purpose of securing the Mediterranean trade. A continuation of this movement possibly had some connection with the invasion of Egypt about 2000 by the Hyksos, whom some authorities regard as Amoritic tribes dislodged from Mesopotamia by the advancing Kassites and Mitani; but their racial affinities are at present obscure.

The Hyksos dominion was destroyed about 1580 B.C. In the fifteenth century all movements were effectively checked by the Egyptian kings, Thutmose I. and his successors, who held Syria up to the Euphrates. Invading movements began again when Egypt became weak at the close of the eighteenth dynasty, about the middle of the fourteenth century B.C.

The Hittites, a people certainly of Alpine race, began to move south from Cappadocia about 2000 B.C., at all events they were warring against Babylon in the eighteenth century (**19,** 425); a Hittite dynasty flourished at Mitani 1420-1411, and in the fourteenth and thirteenth centuries they conquered and largely occupied Syria (**19,** 429). In the middle of the fourteenth century the Khabiri or Hebrews ("robbers"), forerunners of the Aramæan migration, swarmed into Syria from the desert as we know from the Tel el-Amarna tablets. This movement is perhaps to be identified with the conquest of Canaan described in the Book of Joshua.

There was great unrest in eastern Europe and western Asia in the latter half of the second millennium B.C., arising from a southward and eastward shifting of European peoples, affecting both Greece and Asia Minor ; among the most powerful of these invaders were the Phrygians. The Hittite Empire was broken up by these movements about the beginning of the twelfth century. About the same time we find movements from the Ægean to Cyprus and the Syrian coast which introduced the Philistines and other peoples into Palestine. The fall of the Cretan civilisation was doubtless connected with these

changes in the eastern Mediterranean. North
Africa was also involved in these disturbances,
for the Libyans warred with the Egyptians in the
Delta, and employed northern " sea-peoples " to
attack Egypt.

About the ninth-eighth century B.C., the fourth
great Semitic movement began, the so-called
Arabian migration, which culminated in the Islamitic
expansion of the seventh century A.D. (**20,** 4).
The last phase was far-reaching in its effects, not
only western Asia, but the whole of northern
Africa and even southern Europe being implicated
(pp. 58, 46).

Political and national events caused many upheavals in Asia Minor—the indigenous " Alpine "
population, of whom the Hittites were the most
prominent, was fringed by a coastal population of
Mediterranean stock, and the upheavals to the
south added to the general unrest. A potent
ferment was introduced when about 750 B.C. the
Cimmerians (Gimirrai) and Scythians came from the
east. Sargon repelled them with effort in 720, and
they retired westward into Asia Minor, where they
united with a similar band in 710 coming from the
Bosphorus, and established a reign of terror ; they
disappeared at the end of the seventh century.
Keane states (**3,** 280) that the " Kimmerians, Mandas,
Medes with their modern Kurd and Bakhtiari

representatives, were all one people, who were almost certainly of Aryan speech." The country is still terrorised by the Kurds. Before the end of the Byzantine Empire, emigration and deportation had reduced the population of the plateau of Anatolia to one-half. Hordes of Turkoman nomads followed the Seljuk and Ottoman conquests, and by the eleventh century A.D. had become old inhabitants of the eastern Taurus. In succeeding centuries other Turkomans and Kurds followed (8, 247). Thus though there have been many minor shiftings of allied peoples, no serious racial displacement appears to have occurred during the present era ; indeed the Armenians may be regarded as the modern representatives of the Hittites (21).

The Turkish dominance of the Oxus region in the middle of the sixth century A.D. resulted in a westward migration of Turki tribes across northern Persia into Asia Minor. The Seljuk Turks effected a permanent occupation of that region in the latter part of the eleventh century, and this was followed by the dominance of the Osmanli Turks, who, after Orkhan's death in 1359, spread to the Balkan peninsula (p. 47).

The greater part of Iran (p. 12) was originally inhabited by the broad-headed Alpines, who are still represented by the Tajiks, but in Susiana there was in ancient times—and traces still persist—a low-typed dark race, which is usually regarded as allie_ to the Pre-Dravidian stock of south India, or which may have been a true Negroid stock. From the Eur-Asian steppes came Proto-Nordics (p. 16), who became known to history as Medes and Persians, but Semitic migrations have modified the type of the latter as did incursions of tribes allied to the Turki. Some authorities, such as Ripley, see in the dark, dolichocephalic Persians, especially the Lori, a strong Mediterranean strain, while the Farsi are relatively blond dolichocephals, the " Aryans " of many authors. Very numerous peoples have at one time or another passed through or settled in south-western Asia, and it is not to be wondered at that the racial ethnology of this area is perplexing.

So far as is known the bulk of the population of India has been stationary. The oldest existing stratum is that represented by various Pre-Dravidian jungle tribes. The Dravidians may have been always in India : the significance of the Brahui of Baluchistan, a small tribe speaking a Dravidian language, is not understood, probably it is merely a case of cultural drift. The Munda-speaking peoples (Munda, Bhumij, Ho, etc.) are stated to resemble so closely the Dravidians as to be indistinguishable from them. They appear to have been the original inhabitants of the valley of the

Ganges in western Bengal; after many wanderings, apparently across India (9), they settled mainly in Chutia Nagpur.

The first migration into India of which we have evidence is that of Aryan-speaking peoples, perhaps early in the second millennium B.C. Their entry into the Panjab was a gradual one, probably extending over centuries. They first occupied the fertile lands of the Panjab, their progress south-east being barred by the deserts of Rajputana. For a long time their expansion eastward was hindered by the dense forests which then covered the middle plains, but eventually they spread along the valleys of the Jumna and Ganges. The aboriginal elements were prepotent, and the so-called Aryan conquest was more a moral and intellectual one than a substitution of the white man for the dark-skinned people (10, 60), that is, it was more social than racial.

There is a strongly marked brachycephalic element in the population of western India. Risley (11, 59) believes this to be a result of so-called Scythian invasions, but of this there does not appear to be sufficient evidence. The foreign element is certainly Alpine, not Mongolian, and it may be due to a migration of which the history has not been written.

The history of north India was profoundly affected by ethnic disturbances which had their rise in central Asia. The Saka, the Se (Sek) of Chinese historians, were originally a horde of pastoral nomads, like the modern Turkomans, occupying a territory to the west of the Usun horde (p. 16) and to the north of the river Naryn (Syr Darya) or upper Jaxartes. About 160-150 B.C. they were expelled from their pasture grounds by another similar horde, the Yueh-chi, and compelled to migrate southwards. They ultimately reached India about 150-140 B.C., travelling probably through the Pamirs, Gilgit and the Suwat valley, until they entered the plains of Peshawar. Another branch advanced further to the south, perhaps crossed Sind, and occupied Kathiawar. Pahlava, or Parthians of Persia, and Yavana, or Asiatic Greeks, settled in western India about this time (**12**, 197-9), but the subsequent invasions of Demetrios, Eukratides, and Menander, like those of Alexander and Antiochos the Great, were merely military incursions. The Hiung-nu quitted their pasturages in western China shortly after the construction of the Great Wall of China in B.C. 214, which was built to repel the attacks of these and other peoples, which had been going on for at least a century. They encountered an allied Turki tribe of pastoral nomads, the Yueh-chi, who occupied lands in the province of Kan-suh in north-western China, and whom they ousted between 174 and 160 B.C., causing a multitude of from half a million to a million persons of all ages and both sexes to migrate westward. In the course of their westward migration in search of grazing grounds for their vast numbers of horses, cattle, and sheep, the Yueh-chi traversed the territory of the Usun, whom they defeated, and passed on westwards beyond lake Issyk-kul. A small section (the Little Yueh-chi) diverged to the south and settled on the Tibetan border. The main body then encountered the Saka, and drove them from their pasture grounds. About 140 B.C. the Hiung-nu and Usun drove them southwards to Sogdiana and Bactria, lands to the north and south of the upper Oxus (Amu Darya), the peaceful inhabitants of which were reduced to subjection. Here they became a settled, territorial nation. Kadphises I., chief of the Kushan section, established himself as sole monarch of the Yueh-chi nation about 15 A.D. and Kadphises II. (55-78 A.D.), by destroying the Indo-Parthian power, extended his dominion all over north-western India, as far as Benares, but excluding southern Sind. The collapse of the Kushan power in India occurred about 226 A.D. **(12,** 232-259 ; [1914], 248-278).

Hordes of savage Huna (Hoa or Ye-the), mixed Turki and Mongol peoples under Mongol leadership, moved westwards from the steppes of central

Asia, one stream swept towards the valley of the
Volga in 375 A.D. (p. 44), while the other was
directed towards the Oxus. The latter, who became
known as the Ephthalites or White Huns, overcame
Persia (484 A.D.) and poured into India, carrying
devastation over the plains of the Indus and Ganges
and their crowded cities. They were expelled
about 528 A.D. by a confederation of Hindu princes.
(**12,** 297-300.)

The arrival of the Turks in the Oxus valley
in the middle of the sixth century changed the
situation completely, and about 565 A.D. the White
Huns were destroyed and the Turks annexed the
whole of the Hun empire. About the middle
of the seventh century the pressure of the Mussulmans
of the west began to be felt in India, and this
continued till the accession of Sultan Mahmud
(997-1030 A.D.), by whom the conquest was first
undertaken in earnest ; but these and other dynastic
wars did not materially affect the racial character of
the population.

From very early times inhabitants of India
proper migrated into the rich alluvial plains of
Assam, many of whom mixed with aboriginal
population and formed the semi-Hinduised aborigines. The first Indo-Chinese invasion appears
to have been by Tibeto-Burmans. At the end
of the eighth century A.D. the Shan from the head

waters of the Irawadi began to conquer Assam. At the end of the eighteenth century, when Assam was conquered by the Burmese, Khamti and other branches of the Tai or Shan stock entered the country, as did Chingpo from the upper waters of the Irawadi, who also are constantly moving southward into Burma.

Probably two to three thousand years ago the coast of Burma was occupied by Indonesians and the interior by tribes speaking Mon-Khmer languages. From the north came the ancestors of the Tibeto-Burman and Tai peoples, who within the last fifteen centuries have flooded Indo-China with successive swarms of conquerors, and received through Mon and Khmer channels a varnish of Indian culture. The earliest seat of the Tibeto-Burman-speaking peoples appears to have been the headwaters of the Yang-tse-kiang. There is no proof that the Burmans reached the Irawadi valley before 600 B.C. In the ninth century A.D. Burmans occupied the greater part of the Irawadi and other rivers. The Tai or Shan first appear in history in Yunnan, south-west China, and two thousand years ago small swarms of them entered Burma ; the foundation of the Tai principalities in the Salwin valley took place about the third century A.D. ; a great wave of migration occurred in the sixth century, when they peopled the Shan states. When the Mongol hordes under Kublai Khan, in the latter half of the thirteenth century, conquered Indo-China, the Tai went westwards, overran Burma, and forced the Burmans on the Mons, with whom they fused in the sixteenth century. The Karen clans were originally driven south by the Tai.

The Chinese are a mixed people; at base they belong to an eastern Mongoloid stock, but have assimilated various peoples in the north and south. Some students believe, though without any historical evidence, that the progressive element of the old Chinese civilisation was due to a migration of a semi-cultured people from Chinese Turkestan, or even, in the first place, from further west; indeed, it has been stated that in the regions of north Elam, Bak tribes, ancestors of the Chinese, learned the elements of Babylonian and Elamite culture. Originally they were a pastoral and hunting people, but they became solely agricultural. The rich lands of China have always proved a temptation to the nomadic pastoral Manchu and Mongols, who at various times have dominated the sedentary Chinese. It was as a safeguard against such aggressions that Shih Hwang Ti, founder of the Tsin dynasty (246-210 B.C.), built the Great Wall; the southward movements of the Mongolo-Turki hordes were thus arrested and given a westward direction.

Schurtz, following Bälz, says that " the peculiarity of the Japanese is best explained by an admixture of Malay blood ; it is indeed not inconceivable that the political evolution which began in the south was due to the seafaring Malays who first set foot on the southern islands and mixed with the existing inhabitants and with immigrants from Korea " (**13**, 542). The aborigines, whom the Koreans found in Japan, were the Ainu, apparently an outlier of the Alpine race.

Speaking broadly, there has been a continual movement of peoples from south China, mainly in a southerly direction, which has also affected the East Indian Archipelago. These desirable islands have been occupied from very early times by many peoples. During the human period many, if not all, of the islands have been connected, for it is only in a few places that really deep water occurs, and there is reason to believe that the earlier immigrants walked across by land bridges.

The first inhabitants were probably a black woolly-haired race, of which the pygmy representatives (Negritos) are the Andamanese, the Semang of the Malay Peninsula, the Aeta of the Philippines, and the pygmies of New Guinea ; the taller varieties are the recently extinct Tasmanians, who may have walked from New Guinea to Tasmania, the Papuans proper, and the ground stock of the Melanesians.

c

We may regard the next great migration as that of a Pre-Dravidian stock, relics of which are found in the Sakai of the Malay Peninsula, and in a few tribes in the Archipelago. It is now commonly believed that the Australians essentially belong to this stock, having exterminated or amalgamated with the earlier woolly-haired peoples of that continent.

A careful analysis of the mixed population of the East Indian Archipelago indicates that there can be distinguished a dolichocephalic from among the brachycephalic elements (18). The former is best denominated by the term Indonesian. This wave of migration followed—perhaps at a considerable interval—that of the Pre-Dravidian; it probably originated from the lower valley of the Ganges. The southward migrations occurring in south-eastern Asia, to which allusion has just been made, caused Mongoloid brachycephals, who may be conveniently termed Proto-Malays, to overrun the islands, and, as a rule, they have dominated the Indonesians, although, as a matter of fact, even in very early times, a large amount of intermixture appears to have taken place.

The Malay Peninsula was first occupied in the twelfth century A.D. by the true Malays, Orang Malayu, who crossed over from Sumatra ; thence at the close of the thirteenth century they spread over the East Indian Archipelago. But long previously to this other peoples had secured a footing in Java and elsewhere. From the first century of our era there were migrations from India. The Javanese Babads tell of an Indian prince who came to Java about 78 or 120 A.D., where he found a nomadic people. Chinese infiltration probably began long after 220 B.C. when south China was conquered from the aboriginal population and a seaboard acquired, but commercial relations existed with Java and other islands in the fifth century A.D. and were continued for a long period. According to Fritsch (**14,** 14) the Chinese Fa Hien (or Hsien) visited Java in the fifth century A.D. Arabian traders voyaged to the East Indian Archipelago long before the time of Muhammad, but Islam changed the Arab trader into a teacher of the new doctrine ; it was not till the thirteenth and fourteenth centuries that much proselytising was effected, and even so the influence of the Arabs was cultural rather than racial. At the beginning of the sixteenth century the Portuguese made settlements and were followed later by other European peoples.

A mixture of Proto-Malayans with Indonesians, whom we may call Proto-Polynesians, drifted into the west Pacific and gave to the black, woolly-haired natives their language and some elements of higher culture, the resultant mixed peoples being the

Melanesians. Later migrations fared further into the Pacific, probably without delaying their progress through Melanesia, or possibly passing round to the east of it, for only certain Polynesians show traces of Melanesian mixture. The Samoan islands appear to have been their first centre of dispersal within the Pacific, later Tahiti and Raratonga were starting-points for fresh discoveries. An admirable concise account of the wanderings of the Polynesians is given by S. Percy Smith (**7**), who believes that the parent stock can be traced to India about 450 B.C., and that a migration to Java took place in 65 B.C., where they resided for about a hundred years ; but all these early dates are obviously very problematical. In 600 A.D. Polynesians were living in Tonga-nui and Samoa. Hawaii was first settled in 650 and Marquesas was probably occupied twenty-five years later. In 850 New Zealand was visited ; various voyages thither took place subsequently which culminated in the definite occupation of New Zealand by " the Fleet " in 1350. Hawaii was revisited in 1100 and 1225, but all voyages to that group ceased after 1325 till the islands were rediscovered by Captain Cook. Some idea of the enterprise of these remarkable navigators in their sailing canoes may be gathered from the fact that, inspired by the voyage of Ui-te-rangiora to the Antarctic seas in 650, Te Aru-tanga-nuku three hundred years later sailed in search of

the wonders of the deep. He reached the land of
snow and described icebergs, sea-elephants, and the
long fronds of the bull-kelp. Even the remote Easter
Island was colonised, but there is no evidence that
Polynesians reached the coasts of America.

1. KROPOTKIN, P. *Geog. Journ.*, xxiii., 1904, pp. 176, 331, 722.
2. HUNTINGTON, E. *The Pulse of Asia*, 1907.
3. KEANE, A. H. *Man Past and Present*, 1899.
4. MONTEFIORE, A. *Brit. Ass. Rep.*, 1895, p. 828.
5. KENNEDY, J. *J. R. Asiatic S.*, Oct. 1909, p. 1107.
6. WINCKLER, H. *The World's History* (ed. Helmolt), iii., 1903,
   p. 1.
7. SMITH, S. PERCY. *Hawaiki : the original home of the Maori*,
   1904.
8. HOGARTH, D. G. *The Nearer East*, 1902.
9. GRIGNARD, F. A. *Anthropos*, iv., 1909, p. 1.
10. CROOKE, W. *The North-Western Provinces of India*, 1897.
11. RISLEY, H. H. *The People of India*, 1908.   [Ed., 1914.
12. SMITH, VINCENT A. *The Early History of India*, 1908 ; Third
13. SCHURTZ, H. *The World's History* (ed. Helmolt), ii., 1904,
    p. 535.
14. FRITSCH, G. *Globus*. xci., 1907, p. 18.
15. SZINNYEI, J. *Finnisch-ugrische Sprachwissenschaft*, 1910.
16. MEYER, E. *Sitz.-Ber. k. preuss. Akad. d. Wiss*, 1908, p. 656.
17. UJFALVY, C. DE. *Les Aryens au nord et au sud de l'Hindou-
    Kouch*, 1896.
18. HADDON, A. C. *Arch. per l'Antrop. e l'Etnol.*, xxxi., 1901,
    p. 341 ; an Appendix to Hose and Mac-
    Dougall's *The Pagan Tribes of Borneo*, 1912.
19. BREASTED, J. H. *A History of the Ancient Egyptians*, 1908.
20. WINCKLER, H. *Auszug aus der Vorderasiatischen Geschichte*,
    1905.
21. LUSCHAN, F. VON. *Journ. Roy. Anth. Inst.*, xli., 1911, p. 221.
22. RIPLEY, W. Z. *The Races of Europe*, 1900.

CHAPTER III

THE climatic and geographical changes that have taken place in the recent geological history of Europe are dealt with in many books on European geology, but it may not be superfluous to recall to the reader's mind a few of the more salient modifications that have occurred. During a considerable portion of the Glacial age Scandinavia, north Russia, north Germany and the British Isles, except the south of England and probably the south-west of Ireland, were covered by the ice-cap, and confluent glaciers covered the higher mountain ranges to the south. The great Hungarian lake was separated from the Eur-Asiatic Mediterranean (Euxine-Caspian-Aral Sea) by the glaciers of the Carpathians. Between these lakes and the ice-cap there was a variable amount of tundra and steppe-land stretching from western Europe to central Asia. The Mediterranean consisted of a western and an eastern lake, the latter extending over the plains of Lombardy. The western European lands and the remaining portion of Italy were connected with northern Africa by two broad land-bridges. An elevated land surface extended from the western plateaus of Asia to the confines of north Italy.

As the ice retreated the former narrow zone between the ice-cap and the rapidly shrinking central lakes became increasingly habitable tundras and steppes, and was the area of characterisation of the Nordic race, who for a long time were geographically cut off from their neighbours to the south. The then forested and fertile uplands of the Balkan Peninsula and Asia Minor were similarly isolated from the north and south. The gradually increasing Mediterranean never entirely cut off communications between south Europe and north Africa.

Although the archæology of Europe has been better studied than that of any other portion of the old world, we cannot yet recover the complete history of its peoples. It is impossible to deal profitably with periods preceding the Palæolithic age, the earliest phase of which was marked by rude stone implements, of which the counterparts are found widely spread in Africa and are numerous as far as south India. No indication exists as to whether these were fashioned by the same race of men, though it is permissible to suppose that Europe was entered from the south. Several races of men existed in Europe in Palæolithic times, of which the Mousterian or Neanderthal race was the least

specialised. Remains of a race exhibiting certain
Negroid features have been found in a cave at
Grimaldi, near Mentone. Ivory statuettes of palæolithic age indicate that some of the population at all
events possessed the great development of fatty tissue
(steatopygy) which is characteristic of the Bushmen.

After the close of the Palæolithic period the main
existing races of Europe began to appear. Various
branches of the Mediterranean race first spread over
southern and western Europe and the British Islands
as Neolithic man. The pygmy dolichocephals of
Neolithic times, whose remains have been found in
Switzerland, may possibly be representatives of a
race that has disappeared, leaving traces of its short
stature in other countries. During the Neolithic period
the forerunners of the Alpine race expanded westwards along the mountainous forest-zone of Europe
and up the valley of the Danube, and settled in
central France. The Northern, or Nordic, race
extended into western Europe later. As in western
Asia, so in Europe, the Alpine race consists of short
and tall stocks. On the whole, this race has kept
faithfully to its upland habitat, but in Neolithic
times members of it spread across western Germany
to Denmark and south-western Norway, coming
in contact with the tall, fair dolichocephals of the
Northern race. Thus in north-central Europe a
tall, broad-headed people arose who brought the

fashion of erecting round barrows into Britain.
According to Rice Holmes (1, 424-454) bronze was
brought to Britain by more typical members of the
Alpine race, possibly about 1800 B.C., and the first
of various invasions of Keltic-speaking peoples
probably arrived here about 800 B.C. The Umbrians
passed south into Italy during the bronze age, but
were checked and driven up into the Apennines by
the rise of the Etruscan power early in the first
millennium B.C. The Etruscans are said by tradition
to have come from Lydia, but this may have been
mainly a cultural drift.

The mixed peoples of Northern and Alpine descent,
in which the Northern blood predominated, appear
to have possessed exceptional virility. The ancient
writers indiscriminately termed them Keltoi, and
described them as tall, fair-haired, and grey-eyed (2).
The earliest historical movement of this stock was
that of the Achæans, who about 1450 B.C., with their
iron weapons mastered the bronze-using inhabitants
of Greece. Later the Cimmerians, whom we are not
justified in calling Kelts, from their home north of the
Black Sea wandered into Thrace and crossed over
to Asia Minor, others, when hard pressed by the
Scythians, passed round the east side of the Black
Sea to Asia Minor (p. 24). Keltic-speaking peoples
during long periods swarmed across the Rhine into
France, and were there firmly established at latest

by the seventh century B.C. They are believed to
have occupied Spain at the beginning of the sixth
century B.C., and about the same time may have
made their first appearance in Italy. A later and
much more important wave, shortly before 400 B.C.,
broke up the Etruscan power and took Rome
(390 B.C.).

A repetition of earlier movements westwards
across the Rhine is to be found in the case of the
Belgæ, a Kelto-Teutonic people, who considerably
before the first century B.C. occupied the north-
eastern part of Gaul and about the same time
acquired part of the south of Britain.

Volcæ was the name originally applied to a
Keltic-speaking people in west Germany; they
ultimately moved to the south of France and elsewhere. Their name is important as it came to be
used by Teutonic peoples for foreigners of Keltic
nationality as in the cases of Old High German,
Walhā, Anglo-Saxon Walas, and our words Wales
and Welsh.

Thenceforward the great movements in and from
northern Europe were mainly those of purely
Teutonic peoples.

The Cimbri, neighbours of and probably akin to
the Teutoni (7, 214), driven from the north of
Denmark, it is said, by inundations, made their
way into the Danube valley, then turned west and

ravaged Gaul; finally, they invaded Italy and were destroyed by the Romans in 101 B.C.

During the last two or three centuries before the Christian era the Teutonic peoples appear to have been pressing the Keltic peoples across the Rhine; this movement was stopped by the Romans from the time of Julius Cæsar onwards. Augustus actually reduced the whole of west Germany, but after his time the Romans had to be content with the Rhine as their frontier. In the latter part of the second century A.D., the Teutonic pressure became formidable on the Danube frontier, to which the campaigns of Marcus Aurelius gave a temporary relief. Not long afterwards the Goths were moving in a south-easterly direction, and early in the third century A.D. came in conflict with the Romans in the neighbourhood of the Black Sea. In the fourth century, when the Roman Empire was weak, the Goths, Vandals, and other Teutonic peoples made their way into the Balkan Peninsula and adjacent regions. Early in the fifth century the Vandals moved westwards, overran Gaul and Spain, and formed a kingdom in the north of Africa (429 A.D.). The result of this movement of the Vandals was that the Roman frontier in western Germany was destroyed, and the Alemanni and Bavarians pushed their way southwards as far as the Alps. A few years later the Visigoths penetrated into Italy and

captured Rome in 410 A.D.; thence they moved into
the south of France and Spain, where their kingdom
lasted until the beginning of the eighth century.

In the second quarter of the fifth century A.D.,
the Romans had to abandon all their territories west
of the lower Rhine to the Franks, who for some three
quarters of a century or more had been pushed westwards by the Saxons. The Frankish movements
were brought to a head by Clovis, who towards the
end of the fifth century succeeded in conquering
almost the whole of Gaul. About 507 he deprived
the Visigoths of southern Gaul of most of their
possessions. These and other movements of peoples
in Europe during the present era are shown in a
series of admirable maps compiled by Petrie (3).

Huns, coming from central Asia (p. 29), appeared
in Europe in the latter part of the fourth century,
and were welded by Attila into a powerful kingdom
in central Europe. They conquered all the Teutonic
peoples in this region, and through pressure from
them the Burgundians were forced to move westwards into the east of France (c. 443 A.D.). The
disruption of the Huns resulted from their defeat at
Châlons in 451 and Attila's death in 453. Shortly
after this the Ostrogoths, who had been subject to
the Huns, began to assert their strength against the
Romans. Under their king Theodoric they conquered Italy (489-493), where their kingdom lasted

till about 554. In the meantime other Teutonic
nations had been coming southwards to the Danube
region, among them the Langobardi, who by this
time had settled in what is now Austria. Some time
in the sixth century a new wave of invasion spread
from Asia, known as that of the Avars. They swept
across Russia, driving Bulgars, Slavs, and others
before them, till they reached the lower Danube,
on the left bank of which Justinian gave them land.
In 562 they fought with the Franks on the Elbe.
Langobardi and Avars combined and crushed the
Gepidae, who were dominant after the departure of
the Ostrogoths (8, 24), and in 567 the Langobardi,
under their King Alboin, moved into Italy, where
they permanently settled. This was the last of the
great Teutonic migratory movements. The Avars
were thus left in command of the greater part of the
Danube valley. Later, with the Slavs, who had
reached Hungary across the Carpathians in the
sixth century, they overran the Balkan Peninsula,
nearly capturing Constantinople in 625 ; they were
finally crushed in 796 by Pippin I. of Italy, acting for
Charlemagne. In 635 the Bulgars, who had come
with the Huns from the south Russian steppe, revolted from the Avar dominion and subsequently
crossed the Danube into the Balkan Peninsula and
effected settlements in Italy in 680. The Hunagars
had advanced from the Urals to the Volga in 550,

and reached the Danube about 886. Joined by the Magyars and other Turki tribes they dominated the Slavs, and founded the kingdom of Hungary in Pannonia, which absorbed all that remained of the successive Hun and Avar empires of the fifth and sixth centuries (4, 345-6). The westward migration of Asiatics into Europe ceased about the seventh century ; their advance was for the future directed into Syria and along the north coast of Africa, but in the eighth century the Arabs with Berbers pushed into Spain and France from Mauretania, and later made incursions into other Mediterranean countries.

We have seen that the British Isles were early inhabited by a branch of the Mediterranean stock (p. 40), and were subsequently conquered by invasions of Keltic-speaking peoples. In the third century A.D. Teutonic peoples appeared in the British seas, and this movement increased in intensity during the following centuries, bringing the Jutes, Saxons and Angles from Denmark into our country. About the same time the Saxons were raiding in Normandy and Picardy, and established themselves about Bayeux (451). From the end of the eighth century onwards we find a series of maritime movements, often on a large scale, from Scandinavian countries. They brought about Scandinavian settlements in the British Isles in the course of the ninth century, and on the north coast of

Europe, especially in Normandy. At the same time other movements spread across the Baltic, the chief settlements being Kief and Novgorod, which led ultimately to the foundation of the Russian Empire by the Varangians in the course of the tenth century.

The Turks approached Europe from south of the Caspian Sea : in 1063 the Seljuks had crossed the Euphrates and in 1084 occupied Asia Minor ; Jerusalem was captured in 1071. After the lapse of two centuries the Osmanli or Ottomans (p. 25) began a fresh advance from Phrygia, gradually establishing themselves in the Balkan Peninsula ; Macedonia was occupied in 1373, in 1385 they extended northwards and took Sophia, in 1453 Constantinople was taken, and in 1460 the Morea. Nearly a century later they conquered Hungary, which was under Turkish dominance from 1552 to 1687.

The Slavs, who belong to the Alpine race, seem to have had their area of characterisation in Poland and the country between the Carpathians and the Dnieper ; they may be identified with the Venedi. Lefèvre (**5,** 156) emphasises the mixture of races embodied in the Slavs, between whom and the Germanic peoples constant overlapping has taken place. The great south and west movements of the Teutonic peoples were followed by corresponding advances of Slavonic tribes, who spread across the

Oder and Elbe and down the Vistula to the Baltic. Their wide distribution over north-east Germany by the sixth century is attested by place-names. During the last millennium the German language has regained the ground lost, but the broad-headed Slavic type persists (**10**, p. 239). The south-west-ward expansion of the Slavs had by the end of the sixth century carried them across Bohemia as far as the eastern Alps ; thence they went across Pannonia and Illyria to the Adriatic, and in combination with the Avars occupied most of the Balkan Peninsula. By about the ninth century they had extended across the area occupied by the Finns and established them-selves at Novgorod, and apparently penetrated to the Oka and Upper Volga. Their northward expansion was uninterrupted, but in the south-east it was checked by the advent of the Turks. The southern division of Slavs was cut off from the northern by the Magyar empire and later by the growth of the Roumans (**9**, 35).

This general survey of movements shows that the prehistoric trend of Asiatic peoples from east to west has been continued during the first millennium of our era by steppe peoples, in this case arriving north of the Caspian ; the Osmanli, who came in somewhat later, alone followed the old route of the Alpine race. Although the hordes of Asiatic nomads made a pro-found impression in Europe and led to many movements of population, only in relatively few places did they effect permanent settlements. The Northern race, once settled along the shores of the Baltic and North Sea, constituted a fresh source of disturbance. They were a people lightly attached to the soil, and streams of migration radiated west and south ; there was no special inducement to move east, and in any case advance in that direction was checked by invasions from Asia. On the other hand, the occurrence of gold in Ireland and the rich soil of France and northern Italy were strong attractions for migrating west and south. The Alpine peoples had developed the art of metal-working, first in bronze and later in iron, and, having command of the trans-European trade-routes, had advanced in civilisation. Their culture profoundly affected the Nordic tribes with whom they came in contact, and with whom they mixed to a greater or less extent. It is these (to whom the term Kelt may be best applied) who formed the vanguard of the migrations from northern Europe. It is interesting to note that, despite all the movements which have taken place, the distribution of the racial elements in the population of Europe is very similar to that of late Neolithic times (**6,** 9).

1. Holmes, T. Rice. *Ancient Britain and the Invasions of Julius Cæsar*, 1907.

2. Ridgeway, W. Art. "Celts," in *Encycl. Brit.*, Ed. xi., 1910–11.

D

3. PETRIE, W. M. FLINDERS.   *Journ. Anth. Inst.*, **xxxvi.**, 1906.
4. KEANE, A. H.   *Man Past and Present*, 1899.
5. LEFÈVRE, A.   *Germains et Slaves*, 1903.
6. FEIST, S.   " Europa im Lichte der Vorgeschichte," *Quell. u. Forsch. z. alten Gesch. u. Geog.*, 19, 1910.
7. CHADWICK, H. M.   *The Origin of the English Nation*, 1907.
8. VAMBÉRY, A.   *Hungary* (The Story of the Nations), 1887.
9. BEDDOE, J.   *The Anthropological History of Europe*, 1893.
10. RIPLEY, W. Z.   *The Races of Europe*, 1900.

CHAPTER IV

AFRICA

SPEAKING broadly, Africa consists of a great plateau of varying elevations, almost everywhere over 1000 feet high, with broader or narrower coastal lowlands. The edge of the plateau frequently rises into discontinuous mountain-chains, hence few of the rivers are navigable for any great distance on account of rapids. The great area of rainfall and consequent rich vegetation extends roughly from Gambia to the Nile at Sobat junction, then south to the west of the eastern mountain zone as far as the Zambezi; it thus includes the whole Congo basin, and is most intensive north of the Gulf of Guinea and in the upper Congo basin. North and south of this we pass to park scenery, grass steppes, and ultimately to deserts. The coast lands from Morocco to Tunis, and again in the extreme south-east, become more fertile. These conditions profoundly affect the occupations and movements of the population.

De Preville in his brilliant generalisation (1) divides Africa into four zones: (1) The northern deserts, characterised, passing from north to south, by horses, camels, goats, cows. (2) The eastern mountains, the plateaus of which are occupied by pastoral peoples, while hunting, collecting, and cultivation are practised in the valleys and lowlands. (3) The southern steppes, consisting of a northern and eastern margin of bush veld, which merges into grass veld and finally into the western desert. The more favourable lands support people who combine a pastoral with an agricultural mode of life ; in the poorer regions the peoples are simply herders or hunters. (4) The tropical forests, inhabited by hunting peoples and those employed in petty agriculture. In the southern Congo region manioc is largely grown ; north of this the banana is a staple food. On the northern watershed of the Congo the grain-bearing grass eleusine is grown, while in the drier districts to the north dura (Indian millet or Guinea corn) is cultivated.

Africa affords a striking example of the general rule that the more a people is concerned with a pastoral life the more mobile it is, and on the other hand that sedentary habits are induced by cultivation of the soil ; there is, therefore, a tendency for agriculturists to become passive and to be overlorded by the more energetic herders. Petty agriculture alone obtains in the tropical forest area ; in the more open lands, beyond the range of the tsetse fly, the Bantu represent all transitions between a purely nomadic pastoral and a purely agricultural people, according to local conditions. The wide expansion of peoples of this stock may be largely attributed to this combination. Apart from any considerations as to the desiccation of regions of Africa, the natural increase of population would cause the herders of the small plateaus to debouch into neighbouring lands, the agricultural inhabitants of which would be readily conquered by a people whose superior organisation and mobility have been created by their mode of life. The aversion of the true herder to manual labour is a potent incentive to conquest, for example the cow-people (BaHima) have dominated the aborigines of Enkole and the BuNyoro of Uganda (2) in order that these agriculturists may grow millet to make the beer, of which the conquerors drink large quantities. This also accounts for the existence of servile tribes of hunters and smiths in east Africa.

Another inducement to movement, operating in the case of the west African Negro, is the need for salt experienced by purely vegetarian peoples, which in this instance impels them towards the sea. The slave trade, as carried on under Arab influence, has also contributed powerfully to the dislocation of tribes.

Before dealing with individual migrations in Africa a few general considerations are necessary as to the history of man in that continent. In geologically recent times Africa was connected by several land

bridges with Europe, the Red Sea being an inland
lake. Early man could thus wander on foot from one
continent to the other. There is reason to believe
that mankind did not originate in Africa ; but that
all the main races in that continent reached it from
southern Asia. Implements of palæolithic type are
found from Somaliland to the Atlantic, in the Congo
State, and from the Zambezi valley to the Cape. We
know nothing about the men who fashioned these
implements, which are of very great antiquity ; it
is not improbable that we have here indications of a
north and south divarication of Palæolithic man
after he entered east Africa. The next immigration
would seem to have been that of the pygmy folk, who
later specialised into Bushmen and Negrillos ; this
movement was perhaps very little prior to, or contem-
poraneous with, the westerly drift of the primitive
Negro. These short and tall peoples are probably
varieties of one ancient Negroid stock. Even as
late as Ptolemaic and Roman times a nomad people
occupied the desert between the Nile and the Red
Sea : apparently, like the Bushmen and Hottentots,
they were not a black-skinned people (12, 590).

The Bantu-speaking peoples are a mixture of
Negroes with Hamites and in places with other
aboriginal peoples. Stuhlmann (3, 147) terms the
earliest Hamitic arrivals Proto-Hamites, and suggests
that the movement began in the latter part of the

Glacial period. Successive migrations of light-skinned, pastoral Hamites came later. The earliest of these spread all over north Africa, those in the east were the archaic Egyptians, to the west were the Libyans (and their descendants the Berbers) ; those who crossed the Mediterranean formed the European branches of the Mediterranean race. Stuhlmann assumes that Neolithic man in Europe was an immigrant from Africa at the end of the Palæolithic period and did not develop *in situ* from Palæolithic man. He thus supports in the main the well-known views of Sergi (**10**) and Keane (**11**), and as we shall see (p. 56), Elliot Smith gives corroborative evidence that the area of characterisation of this stock was in northern Africa. Another branch gave rise to the Hottentots (p. 61), while later immigrants peopled the Horn of Africa. Himyarites or southern Arabians crossed to east Africa, and true Arabs journeyed by the Isthmus of Suez at various periods from the dawn of history, and in time overran large areas of Africa. At the beginning of history Asiatics came into Egypt, at first from the south, bringing possibly bronze and probably the plough and corn. Later, about 300 B.C., southern Semites settled in Abyssinia (**3**, 48). In the seventh and eighth centuries A.D., Arabs carried the sword and the Koran into Africa and dominated the whole of the northern seaboard. In the ninth century, Jews and Jewish Arab immigrants acquired the domination of Abyssinia ; their descendants are the modern Falasha. Arab, Persian, and Indian influences have also affected the east coast of Africa, and the Arab slave trade has made itself felt throughout tropical Africa.

Professor G. Elliot Smith has demonstrated, mainly from osteological evidence, that more than three thousand years B.C., and we know not how long previously, the whole of Egypt and Nubia was inhabited by a dolichocephalic race of feeble muscular development and slightly below the average stature of mankind. Its members belonged to the small, dark-haired, black-eyed, glabrous group of people, such as are found, on the one side, on the southern shores of Europe, and, on the other, in Arabia. But much as the archaic Egyptian resembles the Mediterranean European and the Arab, he presents an even closer likeness to the Berber (7, 9). In early dynastic times a considerable alien element had already poured into the Delta and was being infused into the Thebaid or Upper Egypt. It was characterised by higher stature, larger and broader head, a narrower and more prominent nose, and greater muscularity. There can be no doubt that this alien element came from the east, most likely from Syria, for the remains of the Christians who came in the sixth century from Syria or Asia Minor and settled about Philæ show similar peculiarities. The

alien element slightly modified the archaic race, and
this mixed type was at first confined to Lower
Egypt, but on the union of the White Crown of
the Thebaid with the Red Crown of Lower Egypt,
a more intimate mixing took place throughout
Egypt, and this blend became the historic or dynastic
Egyptians, the type having undergone remarkably
little change since then. Among the earliest known
pre-dynastic remains from Upper Egypt a certain
number of skulls present variable Negro characters.
Negro influence has always affected Egypt, but it
becomes slighter the further one goes north (23).

Nubia was originally inhabited by the archaic
Egyptians, and it was not till near the time of the
pyramid-builders that any appreciable number of
Negroes came north. Lower Nubia then became the
crucible in which a majority of the old race were
blended with a small but ever increasing number of
Negroes. The eventual product of this mixture is the
Nubian (7, 14). Most of the Negroes who first mixed
with the archaic Egyptians were small, and were
doubtless related to the Bushman or an allied stock.
Tall Negroes also came north in these early times,
but it was not till Egypt loosened her hold on Nubia
(during the Third Dynasty, c. 2980-2900 B.C.) that
the tall Negroes came in any numbers (8, 34-36).
Oetteking (9, 65) has also stated that the racial
elements in Egypt are Bushman, Negro, Libyan,

Hamito-Semite ; he admits a very small percentage
of brachycephaly from some Asiatic source, but does
not specify more closely its place of origin.   The
historical invasions of Egypt were by peoples of
such close physical similarity that the racial type
was little affected by them ; thus the invasions of
the Delta by the Libyans from the west, and the
Mediterranean " sea-peoples " from the north in
the thirteenth and twelfth centuries B.C. (**21, 187**),
made no lasting impression on the population, nor
did the Libyan dominance from 945 to 712 B.C., the
rulers being completely egyptianised (**15,** 364).

According to Keane (**13,** 102) some two thousand
years ago, Nuba (Negroes) migrated from their home
in the Kordofan highlands to the Kargey oasis
(Diocletian's Nobatæ), and others to the Nile about
Meroe (Strabo's Nubæ).   Since then there have
always been Nubians in the Nile valley, mainly in
the region of the Cataracts : they call themselves
Barabra, and have now intermingled with Hamites
and Semites.

Since Neolithic times the Mediterranean race has
occupied Africa north of the Sahara.   Apart from
Phœnician, Roman, and Greek colonies, and the incursions of the Vandals and Alans from Spain, the
only alien racial element has been supplied by the
Arabs, who arrived in the seventh century, and still
remain there.   Some of the Berbers, driven south by

them, developed into powerful desert tribes (*e.g.*
Tuareg).

The Fulani appear to be originally of Berber stock,
and to have drifted south, but by some they are
regarded as of direct Hamitic origin. Wherever they
came from in the first instance, they mixed largely
with the indigenous population. In the early
centuries of our era they were living on the Senegal
River, and were making their presence felt. In the
thirteenth century nomad Cow-Fulani migrated eastward into Hausaland and Bornu, and at the end of
the sixteenth century spread to Lake Chad. Their
gradual invasion of Hausaland during the seventeenth and eighteenth centuries culminated in a
military and political conquest in the early nineteenth century. Thus a pastoral people of non-
Negro origin dominated the Hausa, a distinctly
Negro people. A mixed people of Fulani-Negro
origin, the Jolof, have long constituted the most
important element in Senegambia; they first became known to history in the middle of the fifteenth
century.

From Gambia to Sherboro the western coastland
has constantly received the remnants of peoples
ejected from the Sudan. The Mandingo, another
mixed people of Fulani-Negro extraction but with
Tuareg and Arab infusion (**19, i. 14**), at a remote
period pushed south from the upper Niger through

north-west Liberia and east Sierra Leone ; Mandingo, Kru, and Kpwesi now represent the three main types of Liberia. The Kru migrated to the coast some three centuries ago, retreating before the Mandingo and Fulani ; they first settled about the mouth of the Cavalla River, subsequently advancing westwards. The lowest type of Liberian Negro has been gradually pressed south or enslaved. A steady infiltration of Muhammadan Mandingo from the north continues to influence northern and western Liberia. The Ashanti and Fanti (of the Tshi-speaking group) should be regarded as probably a single people migrating coastward, part of which, the Ashanti, remained beyond the forest belt on the first terraces of the highlands, while the rest, the Fanti, reached the Gold Coast. The Yoruba tribes, who appear to have a non-Negro strain, moved to the Slave Coast from the interior at the beginning of the nineteenth century, driving the Ewe-speaking tribes westwards. The Yoruba movement was caused by the influx of Hausa into the north of their territory, pressed thither by the Fulani (20, 2, 10). The Niger delta harbours remnants of many peoples driven thither by these later arrivals.

The first African home of the agricultural Negroes should probably be sought in the region north of the great lakes, whence they spread over tropical Africa, perhaps pressed westward by the encroaching Proto-

Hamites. The thickset forest Negro represents the more primitive type, while the Nilotic Negro of the open land from the Nile to the Atlantic is tall and long-limbed, in many cases with some infusion of Hamitic blood.

There are still slight traces of an early occupation by the Bushmen of the hunting grounds of tropical east Africa and probably of the country further north (**4**, 421 ; **5**, 514). Thence they gradually drifted south, keeping to the more open grass lands where they could hunt, and at the dawn of history Bushmen were roaming over the whole country south of the Zambezi. The Negrilloes meanwhile became restricted to the great forest areas of the interior ; their southernmost extension is possibly represented by the Kattea of the northern Transvaal.

Contact between Bushmen and Hamites, presumably in the north-east, gave rise to the Hottentots, who shared the pastoral habits of the Hamites and the aversion to agriculture which characterises these herders and hunters like the Bushmen. Thus the Hottentots became pastoral nomadic hunters, stronger than the Bushmen but unable to withstand the Bantu. Their migration from the eastern highlands took place much later than that of the Bushmen. They took a south-westerly course across the savanna country south of Tanganyika, and moved down the west coast till they reached the extreme

south of the continent (16). What is now Cape
Colony was inhabited solely by Bushmen and
Hottentots on the arrival of the Dutch in 1652, who
formed the vanguard of the European colonists.

A branch of the Negro stock blended with Proto-
Hamites in what is now Uganda and British East
Africa, giving rise to the Bantu-speaking peoples,
with some admixture of Negrillo or Bushman
elements. The Bantu are cattle-rearers who
practise agriculture. The more vigorous people
seized the small plateaus which provided pasture,
while the conquered tribes hunted or tilled in the low
country. From these highlands of limited extent
the population overflowed southwards along the
savannas and open country. No data exist for a
history of the early phases of this great expansion,
but we learn from an Arab writer of the tenth
century that Bantu-speaking people had by that
time reached the Zambezi. The detailed history of
these tribes is comparatively recent (5, 6); at the
beginning of the nineteenth century there were
three main groups south of the Zambezi :—

1. The south-eastern group, composed of Ama-
Zulu and AmaXosa, still occupies the plateaus
between the Drakensberg mountains and the
Indian Ocean. They represent the northern and
southern branches of a migration down the east
coast, possibly about the fifteenth century. The

AmaXosa have never crossed the Drakensberg, but about 1800 they spread south as far as Kaaimans River, Mossel Bay, being driven back in 1835 by the colonists to Great Fish River, which had been fixed in 1778 as the boundary between Boers, Hottentots, and Bantu. The AmaZulu have long occupied the coast north of the Tugela River with kindred tribes extending to the Zambezi. Rapid and extensive movements followed the rise of Chaka (1783-1828), for instance the southward flight of the AmaNgwana driving the AmaHlubi before them. About 1817 the AmaNdabili (MaTabili) separated under Umsilikazi, crossed the Drakensberg, and went north-west through the Transvaal, scattering the BeChuana. Repulsed by the Boers, they withdrew to the Zambezi, but were driven out by the tsetse fly. They destroyed the villages of the MaKalanga (MaKalaka) and settled in Mashonaland, pushing the MaShona to north-east.

2. The great central region was occupied very early by Bantu peoples, who drove out or enslaved the Bushmen. At the beginning of last century the pastoral and agricultural forbears of the BaSuto occupied the river beds beyond the Drakensberg, with the aggressive BaTlokua further north ; the more settled agricultural BeChuana lived west of the Marico River, and were expanding by detachments between the Orange River and the Zambezi

and westwards to the Kalahari desert ; and the
MaShona and MaKalanga were to the north-east.
The MaKalanga, after three hundred years' occupation of the country between the Limpopo and the
Zambezi (**17**, i. 291), were conquered by the BaRotse
(apparently allied to the Congo Bantu), who founded
the so-called BaRotse empire on the middle Zambezi.
In 1822 the fierce MaNtati horde (a branch of the
BaTlokua) spread devastation, followed in 1823 by
the tempestuous movement of the allied MaKololo
towards the Zambezi.   Having conquered the
BaHurutse (the dominant BeChuana tribe) and
others, they settled in the fertile uplands beyond
the Zambezi about 1835.   They were driven thence
by the MaTabili into the BaRotse country, the
inhabitants of which subsequently revolted and
exterminated them.

3. The south-western group of Bantu tribes consists of the purely pastoral OvaHerero and the peaceful agricultural OvaMpo to north of them.   The
OvaHerero reached their present home in German
South-West Africa from the east about a century
ago, and drove the Berg Damara south. They
probably represent a branch of the cattle-keeping
south-eastern Bantu, and seem to have advanced
gradually along river beds, their final direction being
due south from the Kunene.

Relatively little is known about the migrations

which have taken place within the vast area of the interior between the Zambezi and the Equator ; three points may be noted, however, in regard to recent movements.

1. A mother-state with offshoots is met with ; for example the Lunda kingdom, north-west of the BaRotse empire, has been the starting-point of various movements : the BaNgala and MaKosa have spread westwards, the BaKete and other tribes northwards (**6,** 64).

2. In equatorial Africa there have been two lines of movement : certain Congo tribes have come southwards, for example the BaYanzi and the BuShongo (BaKuba), with whom were associated the BashiLele and the BaKongo, also the WaRegga and BaKumu further east between the Congo and the Great Lakes. Mr Torday traces the BuShongo now living between the Kasai and the Sankuru to a northern home on the Shari River near Lake Chad. On the other hand, there has been a northward movement on the part of such tribes as the BaPende, BaJok, BaLua, BaBunda and others. The BaLuba went north-west towards the middle Kasai, where they are known as BashiLange. A part of the BaLuba went south from their home on the Lualaba and then east to Kazembe on the Luapula (**18,** 857 ff.). The BaTetela of the Lomani are pressing on the tribes to the west.

E

3. From Guinea to the Kunene there has been a coastward movement, seen in the case of the BaNaka, Fan, BaKalai, and others. The same tendency is manifest in the great Jagga (Imbangala, according to Torday) migration of the fifteenth and sixteenth centuries (**6**, 75).

As regards earlier migrations, tradition points to successive waves of people advancing from north-east Africa to Angola by various routes : they would collect about different centres, which became the starting-point of fresh movements, as seen above in respect to the Lunda kingdom. One early advance from east to west of which some details are known is that of the Jagga, a warlike people whom Barthel regards as akin to the MaSimba. Their starting-point in 1490-1 was about the headwaters of the Congo, whence they streamed westward, temporarily checked with the help of the Portuguese but causing an upheaval in the heart of Africa, in which Lunda was involved, and subduing part of Angola. About the middle of the sixteenth century they were defeated, and the remainder eventually settled near the upper Kwango. They were long the terror of the country at the Congo mouth, and in 1590-1600 raided into Benguela.

The eastern side of the continent, as we have seen, has been a great highway of migration from the north since early times. The MaSimba outbreak of the sixteenth century has many parallels in later history. The MaSimba appeared on the lower Zambezi in 1540, and a long struggle ensued with the MaKalanga helped by the Portuguese, the MaSimba triumphing over both. They pushed north towards the rich towns of the coast, captured Quiloa and Mombasa, but were defeated before Malindi ; subsequently they disappeared from history.

The colonisation of south Africa by Europeans caused a reflex movement of native tribes northwards, while Hamitic incursions from the north were disintegrating the Bantu districts of east Africa. Thus contemporaneously we find the Zulu movement in the south and the Masai advance from the north. The MaSitu set out from the Landin country to south of the Zambezi ; they became entirely zuluised, and formed the northernmost outpost of the Kaffirs to north-west of Nyassa, whence they raided southwards between Nyassa and Bangweolo in the sixties. In 1850 one branch, the WaTuta or ANgoni, moved northward and then north-westward to Ujiji in 1858, then northward again to Urundi and as far as the southern shore of Victoria Nyanza. After a short stay, they moved south to Usukuma about 1860, and were finally conquered by the zuluised WaNyamwesi under Mirambo, and given land in the north-west of their country. The

WaHehe, also known as the MaFiti, are a branch of the MaSitu ; they raided through Ugogo and Usagara to the coast until the Germans intervened.

Early in the Christian era there was an influx of pastoral Hamitic peoples into the eastern Horn of Africa, the first to arrive being the Galla (Oromo), who occupied the southern edge of the Gulf of Aden in pre-Islamitic times. The Galla pushed into the Abyssinian highlands, while the Somâl in their rear spread southwards from the Gulf of Aden. The Danakil (or Afar) probably crossed the Strait of Bab-el-mandeb later and spread thence into their present home between the Abyssinian mountains and the Red Sea. The Somâl have steadily spread west and south to more fertile country, causing Galla tribes to retreat down the coast and then, when checked by the Masai in the south, along the valley of the Juba and up its tributaries towards the northwest. The campaigns of Muhammad Granj in the early sixteenth century profoundly affected the stratification of peoples in this part of Africa, resulting in the intermingling of Hamitic elements with the Semites, Negroes, and Bantu, whence arose the Masai, BaHima, and other tribes in the Nile lakes area (**14, i**. 20). Remnants of conquered peoples in several instances survive as pariah tribes.

The Masai, representing a fusion of Hamites with Nilotic Negroes, are an aggressive pastoral tribe with

a military organisation hardly surpassed by that of
the Zulus. From the region north-east of Victoria
Nyanza they have spread south, driving out the
agricultural peoples. Their great inducement has
been cattle-raiding. Parts of Usagara, German East
Africa, have been devastated by both Masai from
the north and MaFiti from the south. Since 1891 the
rinderpest, together with the influence of the white
man, have reduced the wealth and power of the
pastoral peoples, giving the agriculturists a chance of
recuperation.

In the neighbourhood of Victoria Nyanza the pastoral BaHima, of Hamitic—probably Galla—descent,
dominated the indigenous Bantu and intermingled
with them between the fourteenth and sixteenth
centuries (to judge from the genealogy of the kings
of Uganda). Their centre of dispersion was Unyoro,
east of Albert Nyanza (4, 449), and they spread
over Uganda and Karagwe to Urundi, where they
were called WaTusi. They have scattered across
Unyanyembe as far as the western edge of Ugogo.

The obscure ethnological history of Madagascar is
succinctly dealt with by Mr T. A. Joyce in an in-
valuable handbook (22, 245). The aborigines were
negroid; some authorities believe that these were
Oceanic negroids (Melanesians) and not African
Negroes, though numbers of Bantu slaves have been
brought over by Arabs. From Pre-Muslim times

various groups of Arabs have arrived and imposed themselves on the population. The southern end of the island has been affected by Indian immigration. The Antimerina (" Hova ") migrated from the East Indian Archipelago, and landed on the east coast about four centuries ago, and became dominant in the seventeenth century.

On taking a general survey of the racial history of Africa it is manifest that the critical area is the north-eastern region, which abuts on southern Arabia. It was here that most of the peoples must have entered Africa, the remainder coming across the northern boundary of the Red Sea. As all the later immigrants were pastoral peoples, the desert band to the north of the southern route, threaded only by the narrow and densely populated Nile valley, prevented extensive movement northwards. The forests of the basin of the Congo, and its affluents arrested all migrations of pastoral peoples as such ; two routes alone lay open : one to the west in the open country between the desert and the forest, the other southwards down the eastern mountain zone. The latter has been the track of the Bushmen, Hottentots and southern Bantu-speaking peoples, and quite recently the Masai, were following the same route when their progress was arrested by the coming of the white man. There has also been a steady pressure of peoples of Libyan and Berber extraction southwards across the Sahara tending to drive the Negro ever farther south into the forest region. The higher elements in the population of the western Sudan may thus be traced to influences from the north and east.

1. PREVILLE, A. DE. *Les Sociétés Africaines*, 1894.
2. ROSCOE, J. *Journ. Roy. Anth. Inst.*, xxxvii., 1907, p. 93.
3. STUHLMANN, F. VON. *Handwerk und Industrie in Ostafrika*, 1910.
4. SCHURTZ, H. *The World's History* (ed. Helmolt), vol. iii., 1903, p. 395.
5. HADDON, A. C. *Rep. Brit. Ass.* (S. Africa), 1905, p. 511.
6. BARTHEL, K. Völkerbewegungen auf der Südhälfte des afrikanischen Kontinents, *Mitt. des Vereins f. Erdkunde in Leipzig*, 1893.
7. SMITH, G. ELLIOT. *Cairo Sci. Journ.*, iii., 1909.
8. SMITH, G. ELLIOT, AND JONES, F. WOOD. *Arch. Surv. Nubia. Rep.* for 1907-8, ii., 1910.
9. OETTEKING, B. *Arch. f. Anth.*, xxxvi., 1909.
10. SERGI, G. *The Mediterranean Race*, 1910.
11. KEANE, A. H. *Ethnology*, 1896, p. 374. *Man Past and Present*, 1899, p. 450.
12. NIEBUHR, C. *The World's History* (ed. Helmolt), vol. iii., 1903, p. 587.
13. KEANE, A. H. *Journ. Anth. Inst.*, xiv., 1884.
14. PAULITSCHKE, P. *Ethnographie Nordost-Afrikas*, i., 1893.
15. BREASTED, J. H. *A History of the Ancient Egyptians*, 1908.
16. STOW, G. W. *The Native Races of South Africa*, 1905.
17. THEAL, G. M'C. *History and Ethnography of Africa south of the Zambesi* (1505-1795), 3 vols., 1907-1910.
18. TORDAY, E. *Bull. Soc. belge d'Études coloniales* (Brussels), No. 12, 1910, p. 857; and

TORDAY, E., AND JOYCE, T. A.   "Les Bushongo," *Annales du Musée du Congo Belge*, Sér. III., Tome ii., Fasic. i., 1911.

19. JOHNSTON, SIR H.   *Liberia*, 2 vols., 1906.
20. ELLIS, A. B.   *The Yoruba-speaking Peoples*, 1894.
21. CHADWICK, H. M.   *The Heroic Age*, 1911.
22. *Handbook to the Ethnological Collections*, British Museum, 1910.
23. SMITH, G. ELLIOT.   *The Ancient Egyptians*, 1911.

CHAPTER V

AMERICA

THE absence of anthropoid apes from America, at any period of the world's history, clearly precludes the possibility of man's having originated independently in the New World. Even if the anthropoids be collateral descendants with man of a remote common ancestor, still their absence would presuppose the absence also of that common ancestor. The population of America must therefore have come from the Old World. Only two probable routes exist, for we may exclude in human times any landbridge across the mid-Atlantic, and, similarly, there is no reason to believe that the connection of South America with the Antarctic continent persisted during human times. We are therefore compelled to look to a farther extension of land between North America and northern Europe on the one hand, and between north-west America and north-east Asia on the other. We know that in late Tertiary times there was a land-bridge connecting north-west Europe with Greenland, and Dr Scharff (1, 155) believes that the Barren-ground reindeer took this route to Norway and western Europe during early glacial times, but that "towards the latter part of the Glacial period the land-connection . . . broke down " (*l.c.* 186). Other authorities are of opinion that the continuous land between the two continents in higher latitudes remained until post-glacial times. Dr Brinton (8) considered that it was impossible for man to have reached America from Asia, because Siberia was covered with glaciers and not peopled until late Neolithic times, whereas man was living in both North and South America at the close of the Glacial age. He acknowledged frequent communications in later times between Asia and America, but maintained that the movement was rather from America to Asia than otherwise. He was therefore a strong advocate of the European origin of the American race.

Others again see evidence in certain cultural and linguistic affinities of Polynesian migrations into America ; but the Polynesians do not appear to have reached eastern Oceania till towards the close of the seventh century A.D.

Only a narrow strait now separates Alaska from Siberia, and the Aleutian Islands form an almost complete series of stepping-stones across the most northerly part of the Pacific. There is no doubt that North America was connected with Asia in Tertiary times in this direction, but some geologists assert that " the far North-west did not rise from the waves of the Pacific Ocean (which once flowed with a boundless expanse to the North Pole) until after the glacial period." In that case " the first inhabitants of America certainly did not get there in this way, for by that time the bones of many generations were already bleaching on the soil of the New World " (**2,** 181).

The " Miocene Bridge " as the land connecting Asia and America in late geological times has been called (**4,** ii. 61, 344), was probably very wide ; one side would stretch from Kamtchatka to British Columbia and the other across Behring Strait. If, as seems probable, this connection persisted till, or was reconstituted during, the human period, tribes migrating to America by the more northerly route would enter the land east of the great barrier of the Rocky Mountains. The route from the Old World to the New by the Pacific margin probably remained nearly always open.

As in Europe, the northern part of the continent was at one time covered by a great glacial sheet rendering it uninhabitable. This Glacial period belongs to very recent geological times. The ice-sheet spread over practically all Canada, and over New England and New York as far as the Ohio River, and westwards over the prairies and part of the great plains. The chain of great lakes and the lakes and watercourses of central and eastern Canada mark the ragged track of its boundary (**3**, 15). It is obvious that during the period of the great extension of the ice-sheet no immigration could take place into America, except possibly, as already mentioned, from north-east Asia to the Pacific slope of North America along the southern border of the North Pacific Bridge.

Ethnologists are generally agreed as to the similarity of type prevailing among most of the peoples of the New World, which points to an original common parentage. For instance the coarse, lank, black hair is a prevailing characteristic throughout both the northern and the southern continent, and in other respects a resemblance to the Mongoloid type is equally widespread. Thus it is to Asia rather than to Europe that we must look for the first ancestors of the American Indians, though it would not be correct to regard them as a branch of the Mongol race. The number of languages in America is very remarkable, but recent investigations show that there is a closer affinity between some of them than has been hitherto supposed, indeed one writer goes so far as to say that language in America " is the unmistakable voice of a race, echoed through a thousand vernacular dialects " (**4**, ii. 75). The racial problem is not so simple, however, as this would imply, and Deniker (**5**, 509) and Keane (**6**, 353) are probably correct in suggesting that there have been several migrations at various periods from the Old World ; they further agree in postulating migrations from Europe as well as from Asia.

There are indications of a palæo-ethnic and a neo-ethnic period in the New World as well as in the Old ; the interval dividing them may correspond to that dividing pre- or inter-glacial from post-glacial times. It seems likely that certain peoples of low stature, occurring here and there in America, represent the first palæo-ethnic inhabitants of America.

Traces of palæo-ethnic man have been met with in various parts of South America and perhaps in the south of California if ten Kate be correct (**21**). This high and narrow-headed race of the Lagoa-Santa type represents the primordial element of population in South America. Looking at the present distribution of the descendants of this Lagoa-Santa race, we find them all border peoples ; they are to be met with in eastern Brazil, in the south of Patagonia and Tierra del Fuego where the climate is rigorous, in the islands of western and southern Chile, on the Ecuador coast, and apparently in south California. Their distribution seems to indicate that they have been driven out in a great excentric movement from their old habitat, and, with new environment and crossing, fresh variations of the type have arisen. This type is absent throughout the northern part of

South America, and there is a great gap in its
occurrence (except as a fossil or sub-fossil) from
southern Brazil to Patagonia (**7**).   Keane (**6, 353**)
suggests that the long-headed peoples, like the
Eskimo and Botocudo, are descendants of the long-
headed Palæolithic man of Europe, while the broad-
headed Mexicans and Andeans have sprung from a
later and probably much larger section migrating
from eastern Asia.

There is nothing to show how the Lagoa-Santa
race reached South America.   No traces of it have
been recorded east of the Rocky Mountains, but the
negative evidence of the absence of fossil remains
has no especial weight, and the later survivors may
have been exterminated or assimilated by the
ancestors of the existing natives of North America.
So there is no real reason why this race should not
have crossed from Europe by the North Atlantic
Bridge if the way were open.   Or it may have come
from north Asia and kept to the Pacific slope, while
working its way to South America.

The Eskimo will be dealt with later.   The inhabitants of the plains east of the Rocky Mountains
and the eastern wooded area are characterised by a
head which varies about the lower limit of brachycephaly, and by tall stature.   This stock probably
arrived by the North Pacific Bridge before the last
Glacial period, and extended over the continent east

of the great divide. Finally bands from the north, east, and south 'migrated into the prairie area. The markedly brachycephalic immigrants from Asia appear to have proceeded mainly down the Pacific slope and to have populated Central and South America, with an overflow into the south of North America. It is probable that there were several migrations of allied but not similar broad-headed peoples from Asia in early days, and we know that recently there have been racial and cultural drifts between the neighbouring portions of America and Asia. Indeed Bogoras suggests that ethnographically the line separating Asia and America should lie from the lower Kolyma River to Gishiga Bay (**9,** 579).

[*For Bibliography see p.* 95.]

CHAPTER VI

NORTH AMERICA

NORTH AMERICA has the outline of a vast triangle, the base of which extends beyond the Arctic circle, and the apex into the tropics. The land mass possesses a climate which is essentially temperate, but marked by those extremes which characterise a continental area. The low-lying central region of the north passes into the tundra of the frozen north, and no obstacles deflect the icy north winds. The most striking relief feature is the Cordillera, an immense mountain-chain which stretches from Alaska to the south. In reality, it is a great plateau with a breadth of one thousand miles in the United States, and with an elevation of from five to ten thousand feet. Upon this table-land rise various mountain-ranges running longitudinally north and south, mainly along its margins, the central plateau being arid and frequently desert. Eastward from the Cordillera stretches the great central basin bounded on the east by the Appalachian or eastern mountain system. The wooded Appalachians present many breaks and groups. In the north the great central basin is cold and barren ; between latitudes fifty and sixty degrees, it is covered for the most part with forests; while from fifty degrees southward stretch on the west the dry and treeless great plains, and on the east the more fertile plains; southwards the great plains disappear in the richness of vegetation brought about by the increased rainfall of Mexico and Central America (3, 1-22). The great plains are rolling in character, and are intersected by river valleys, which are generally thinly wooded. The plains are drained by the Mississippi and its innumerable affluents. The chain of great lakes forms a noticeable feature of the northern wooded area, and the northern tundras are dotted with lakes of varied size. The Pacific slope has a genial insular climate which marks it off sharply from the rest of the continent.

These physical conditions combined with the absence of contact with great cultural centres have directly affected the economic life of the people. The Arctic peoples could live only by fishing and hunting. Farther south collecting of wild vegetable produce gave increased variety in food, but except on the north-west coast fishing was not practised to any great extent. Horticulture seems to have spread along the great plains and up the eastern wooded area, mainly, if not entirely from the south; but it was never practised along the Pacific slope, and the Californian Indians as a whole remained in a very

F

low state of culture. The marvellous salmon rivers and the drowned valleys of the north-west predisposed the peoples of this highly favoured area to fishing, and various circumstances combined to encourage the development of a special type of culture. Under very different circumstances a peculiar culture was also evolved by the Pueblo Indians of Arizona and New Mexico, but here a cultural drift from Mexico may be suspected.

If man lived in North America during pre- or interglacial times, the earlier inhabitants must have been pressed southwards to more genial climes by the great ice sheet. At the close of the glacial period a movement northwards would begin, the impulse of which would be felt from Mexico to the Atlantic. The relative position of the main stocks from west to east according to Winchell (**10,** 207) would then be approximately as follows : Athapascan, Shoshonean, Algonquian, Caddoan, Muskhogean, Siouan, and Iroquoian. Farrand, however, in common with most American anthropologists considers that " glacial man is doubtful " (**3,** 72).

The Eskimo, or Innuit, occupy more than five thousand miles of sea-board, from north-east Greenland to the mouth of the Copper River in western Alaska. Many views have been advanced as to the position of their centre of dispersion ;

most probably it lay to the west of Hudson Bay. Rink is of opinion (**11**, 3, 32), that they originated as a distinct people in Alaska where they developed an Arctic culture ; but Boas regards them " as, comparatively speaking, new arrivals in Alaska, which they reached from the east " (**22**, 534), A westward movement is supported by myths and customs, and by the settlements of Eskimo in extreme north-east Asia. There was always hostility between the Eskimo and the North American Indians, which, apart from their very specialised mode of life, precluded any Eskimo extension southwards.

The expansion of the Eskimo to Greenland is explained by Steensby (**13**, 392) as follows : the southern main movement would have followed the west coast from Melville Bay, rounded the southern point and proceeded some distance up the east coast. From the Barren Grounds north-west of Hudson Bay the Polar Eskimo followed the musk-ox due north to Ellesmere Land, then crossed to Greenland, and, still hunting the musk-ox, advanced along the north coast and down the east coast towards Scoresby Sound. Another line of migration apparently started from the vicinity of Southampton Island and pursued the reindeer northwards into Baffin Land ; on reaching Ponds Inlet these reindeer-hunting Eskimo for the most part turned along the east coast.

The Athapascans occupied a wide area in the north-west extending from the Rockies almost to Hudson Bay, and also a smaller though far more densely populated territory in the south-west in the states of Arizona, New Mexico, and Colorado. In later times the trend of migration has been from north to south ; in Washington, Oregon and California, small detachments spread westwards to the Pacific coast, but there is no evidence of any expansion eastwards. The northern Athapascans call themselves Déné, the southern representatives of the stock are the Navaho, Apache, with the Hupa of California.

The Shoshonean centre of dispersion lies west of the Rocky Mountains, but these tribes probably did not migrate far. Some Shoshonean tribes formerly east of the Rockies, were pushed south and west by the Blackfeet, and probably they in turn pressed on the Shahaptians of the Columbia valley. The Shahaptians in their movement north and west forced back the Salish on to the northern bank and tributaries of the Columbia. Later the Shahaptians obtained horses and drove back the Snakes (Shoshonean) from the Columbia River.

According to Winchell, who believes that man was pre- or inter-glacial in America (10, 213), the Algonquian stock originated in the south-west, and after the retreat of the ice " spread over the interior plains, and pre-empted the timbered regions of Canada and the northern United States," eventually extending over the breadth of the continent from Montana and Alberta to the Atlantic, and at one time holding most of Canada. In 1000 A.D. they were on the Atlantic coast, for Vikings encountered them (Micmacs) in Vinland, east Nova Scotia (12, 72). Their traditions point to an original home in the north-east, beyond the Great Lakes, whence they had been driven by the Iroquois before the Discovery. They migrated along two lines, one going south-east, along the coast, and up the rivers into the Alleghanies, the other west along the Great Lakes. They were orginally food-collectors, but some of the western tribes learnt agriculture from Mississippi tribes (22, 532). The two branches differentiated during centuries, and it is only by their kindred language, that the relationship of the Shawnee of the south and the Ojibwa of the north is unmistakably shown. The south-east branch of Algonquians, having crossed the Savannah River, encountered strange Indians who checked their further progress in that direction ; they therefore turned west and spread into Tennessee where they were called Savannee or Shawnee.

The Ojibwa (Chippewa) have a tradition that they dwelt on the Atlantic coast north of the St Lawrence about five hundred years ago. They moved thence, stopping on the St Lawrence, Lake Huron, and at Sault Ste. Marie, then finally at La Pointe, Wisconsin. Possibly they were driven west by the Iroquois confederacy, but they are mainly an aggressive people. They split into three divisions. South of Lake Superior they encountered the Foxes (another Algonquian tribe) and Dakota with whom they fought for the possession of the wild-rice district. After some hundred and twenty years they drove out the Foxes and Dakota, and spread south and west. Early in the seventeenth century they traded furs with the French for guns, with the aid of which they drove the Foxes to the Mississippi in 1746. The great incentive for the immigration of these and other tribes into north Wisconsin and east Minnesota was the possession of the wild-rice marshes ; possibly the Foxes and Dakota offered a less stubborn resistance because the plains afforded the counterattraction of bison-hunting. After 1783 the Ojibwa spread over the rest of north Wisconsin and Minnesota (**14**, 1038 ff.).

The Cree are an important Algonquian tribe living in Manitoba and Assiniboia, between the Red and Saskatchewan rivers ; they formerly ranged far to the north, and to the south of Hudson Bay. Like the kindred Ojibwa they were essentially a forest people. There is a tradition that part of the tribe lived about the Red River (Minnesota) with the

Ojibwa, but were attracted to the plains by the bison.

The traditions of the Lenni-Lenape, another Algonquian tribe, state that they came from the north, doubtless west of Lake Superior, " where it was cold and froze and stormed, to possess milder lands abounding in game." Fighting their way, they sojourned in the land of firs, and later arrived on the plains of the buffalo land. Then they " longed for the rich east-land " and their passage across the Mississippi in south Minnesota was contested by the Tallegewi (Tsalagi or Cherokee) ; these were a tall people who had many large towns and fortifications ; they were probably the effigy-builders of the Wisconsin-Minnesota-Iowa region of the old mound-builders. Those who crossed the river, being assisted by the Mengwe (an Iroquoian tribe, Hurons ?), eventually expelled the Tallegewi, who fled down the Mississippi. Most of the Lenape remained in the Mississippi valley, but some finally settled in the eastern states, part of whom were known as Delaware (10, 217).

The Cheyenne still lived in north Minnesota in 1700. They were driven west by the Sioux, who were themselves retiring before the Ojibwa, then already in possession of guns from the east. In 1850 they divided into a northern band which re-mained in Montana, and a southern band which wandered towards Colorado, Kansas and Oklahoma. Originally an agricultural people, they afterwards became typical nomad Plains Indians.

The Blackfeet, or Siksika, till recently ranged from the north Saskatchewan River to the Yellowstone River in Montana, and from the Rocky Mountains to 105° W. long.   According to Grinnell (**15**, 177) they moved from the wooded lake area of Athabasca in the north to the open country to the south, but Horatio Hale believes they came from the Red River country ; in any case " the westward movement of the Blackfeet has probably been due to the pressure of the Crees upon them. . . . They have gradually advanced westward to the inviting plains along the Red River and the Saskatchewan, pushing the prior occupants before them by the sheer force of numbers. This will explain the deadly hostility which has always existed between the Crees and the Blackfeet " (**16**, 700).   It is probable that the people whom they found in possession of the prairie had come through the passes from the country west of the Rocky Mountains, which would account " not only for the peculiarities of the language and character of the Blackfeet tribes, but also for the different traditions which are found among them in regard to their origin and former abode " (**16**, 704).   This migration apparently took place a little over a hundred years ago.

The Caddoan tribes came northwards from the south-west ; the Caddo long lived on the Red River of Louisiana, other branches settled along the rivers of north-east Texas, while the Pawnee migrated to Kansas and Nebraska. The Pawnee practised agriculture more than the other Plains Indians, which is additional evidence of their southern origin, for, judging from the distribution of maize and tobacco, agriculture is admitted to have proceeded northwards from Mexico and Central America.

The Indians who checked the Algonquian advance south, were presumably Muskhogeans whose best known representatives were the Creeks and Chickasaw. They were apparently a people little addicted to migration ; their territory along the rivers flowing into the Gulf of Mexico parallel to the Mississippi, probably represents their ancient home ; in early times it undoubtedly extended farther north, and possibly farther east. Not only did the cultural influence of the Arawak extend to Florida from the Antilles, but there were colonists from Cuba who had come in search of the mythic fountain of youth.

The prehistoric Siouan people were neighbours in the Carolinas of the prehistoric Iroquoians, and the two people, more or less allied in language, and having similar customs and the same opportunities for northward migration, probably moved about the same time (**10,** 214). The Siouans coming down

Big Sandy River reached the Ohio at a point lying on the south-west border of the territory over which the Cherokee expanded. Geographical names confirm the tradition that they settled for some time in the Ohio valley. By the time of the Discovery of America they had extended beyond the Mississippi (**2**, 211).

The course of the later migrations of the Sioux-Dakota can be definitely established ; they came down the Ohio, being driven west by the Algonquians. The stream of retreating Sioux divided into two branches, one going up the Mississippi and the other spreading downstream. The former, consisting of Dakota and others, seems to have encountered a kindred tribe, the Winnebago, in Minnesota and Wisconsin, who were possibly the representatives of an earlier occupation of this area by the Siouans ; at all events the Winnebago dialect is one of the oldest of the Siouan stock in the Mississippi region, and this tribe is called " grandfathers " by the rest. The Sioux fugitives occupied the wild-rice fields of Minnesota and Wisconsin for a time until the Ojibwa penetrated thither and disputed possession with them. The Dakota then took to the plains and became typical bison-hunting Plains Indians. This development was greatly assisted by their acquisition of the horse (**14**, 1044) : it was in the winter of 1802-3 that the Dakota first saw and stole horses wearing shoes. The Winnebago were to such a degree attached to the soil that they remained between the Mississippi and Green Bay, Lake Michigan, living at peace with the surrounding Algonquians.

The Assiniboin or " Stone Sioux " of the Dakota group, had separated from the Sioux probably in the Lake of the Woods region by 1640. In 1658 they were between Lake Superior and Hudson Bay, whence they moved north-west; in 1670 they were living near Winnipeg. They joined the Cree and fought against other Dakota tribes. Finally they moved westward, on to the plains and became nomadic (12, 81).

As to the original home of the Iroquoians nothing is definitely known beyond the fact that they crossed a great river to reach those north-eastern States which they occupied at the Discovery (17, 146). The facts that the " three supporters," beans, maize and squashes, figure in their mythology and that they made use of the blow-gun, as well as linguistic evidence (22, 531), point to their having come from a southern home, though their traditions refer only to their later northern home which they left and crossed the St Lawrence. In historic times they occupied the eastern lake region and the country south and east. The Cherokee represent the first southward wave of Iroquoian migration; they reached the Ohio driving out the Algonquians already settled there, and occupied this region for a considerable time.

Another detachment of Iroquoians, the Huron, moved west, probably before the main Iroquoian migration ; these Huron became absolutely alienated from the parent stock, and bitter enmity subsequently prevailed between the two. North of Lake Erie were the mound-building Attiwandaron, who probably represent the vanguard of the Huron westward migration. The Iroquoians were an aggressive people, and drove the Huron farther west, in the end practically exterminating them, and the Attiwandaron in 1650. Subsequently the Ojibwa gradually took possession of the peninsula of Ontario after a struggle with the Iroquois. When Ontario became British all the Indians within its area were Algonquians. It was pressure from the Iroquois which caused the migration of the Sioux-Dakota to the plains, which took place within historic times.

The Iroquoians were physically the finest of all the Indians, and excelled in warlike qualities. They owe their fame chiefly to their great military organisation of the League of the Five Nations (the Mohawk, Onondaga, Oneida, Cayuga and Seneca), which was joined in 1722 by a sixth, the Tuscarora from the south. The League was definitely constituted about the year 1570 to secure universal peace and welfare among men by the recognition and enforcement of the forms of civil government.

The movements of the Indians, especially of those nearer the coast, were largely affected by the incoming of the French and English after the Discovery, and their distribution was also modified by the warfare between these two peoples. At the present day the Indians are all located in reservations which frequently coincide to some extent with the original habitat of the several tribes.

As previously indicated, the ethnical history of the Pacific slope is entirely different from that of the rest of North America, owing to its geographical and climatic conditions. The population has been essentially a static one, as is demonstrated by the great diversity of languages, although some tribes have percolated across the great divide, while inland tribes have come down to the coast. Only a few examples need be given.

The Salish tribes of the coast probably came from the interior ; the Tillamook apparently crossed over the territory of the Chinook to get to their position on the Oregon coast south of the Columbia River.

The Kutenai Indians of British Columbia, judging from tradition, are comparatively modern intruders in the area now occupied by them, which extends from about 50° N. lat. to northern Idaho and Montana. Their earlier home seems to have been

Alberta about the headwaters of the Saskatchewan (**18,** 179).

The Dieguenos of southern California have migrated there from the southernmost part of Nevada, as is proved by the parallels between their myths with those of the Mohave (**19**).

There is unquestionable resemblance between the Pueblo Indians and their northern neighbours ; in fact, the whole population from Alaska nearly to the Isthmus belongs to one great family, which must have split up very early judging from linguistic dissimilarity.   The separate hall for religious ceremonies, the kiva of the Pueblo Indian, is met with in California as well, so too are the religious mask dances.   The antiquities of the Pueblo region afford evidence of a progressive movement from north to south with some degree of cultural develop- ment, seen especially in the transition from the cliff- dwellings of the central plateau to the pueblos of the Zuñi and Hopi, built on rocky, almost inacces- sible hills.   The migrations of the Pueblo Indians were of necessity slow as they lived almost exclusively by agriculture.

The great Pueblo area between the Rio Pecos and the Colorado never formed a political whole.   Petty feuds between rival communities and the struggle with drought were the undoing of the Pueblo Indians. We know that the Zuñi culture is due to a fusion of two racial elements; the first from the north and north-east, the second, which it shares with other little Colorado pueblos, came from the Gila valley in southern Arizona (**20**, 82). A factor to be reckoned with in considering the movements of people in this region is the increasing dryness of the climate. Hostile tribes pushed the Pueblo Indians farther and farther into the arid steppe-lands, where a special form of fortified village, the pueblo, originated by way of defence against enemies to north and east. The fierce Apaches and Navaho made marauding expeditions to pillage the garnered crops of the Pueblo Indians; the Spaniards found this warfare in full swing, and it must have been going on for generations (**2**, 213-222).

1. SCHARFF, R. F. *The History of the European Fauna,* 1899.
2. HAEBLER, K. *The World's History* (ed. Helmolt), i., 1901, p. 180.
3. FARRAND, L. *Basis of American History,* 1904.
4. PAYNE, E. J. *History of the New World called America,* i., 1892; ii., 1899.
5. DENIKER, J. *The Races of Man,* 1900.
6. KEANE, A. H. *Man Past and Present,* 1899.
7. RIVET, P. *Bull. et Mém. Soc. d'Anth. (Paris),* ix., 1908.
8. BRINTON, D. G. *The American Race,* 1891.
9. BOGORAS, W. *Am. Anth.,* iv., 1902, p. 577.
10. WINCHELL, N. H. *Pop. Sci. Monthly,* lxiii., Sept. 1908.
11. RINK, H. "The Eskimo Tribes, their Distribution and Characteristics," *Meddelelser om Grönland,* Hefte 11, 1887.

12. THOMAS, CYRUS.   *Arch. Rep.* (1905), Toronto, 1906, p. 71.
13. STEENSBY, H. P.   *Meddelelser om Grönland,* xxxiv. 255, 1910.
14. JENKS, A. E.   19*th Ann. Rep. Bur. Am. Eth.* (1897-8), 1900, p. 1011.
15. GRINNELL, G. B.,   *Blackfoot Lodge Tales,* 1892.
16. HALE, H.   *Rep. Brit. Ass.,* 1885 (Aberdeen), p. 696.
17. BOYLE, D.   *Arch. Rep.* (1905), Toronto, 1906, p. 146.
18. CHAMBERLAIN, A. F.   *Arch. Rep.* (1905), Toronto, 1906, p. 178.
19. DU BOIS, C. G.   *XVe Congres international des Américanistes,* no. 28.
20. FEWKES, J. W.   *Putnam Anniversary Volume,* 1909, p. 41.
21. KATE, H. TEN.   *Bull. Soc. d'anth. de Paris,* vii., sér. 3, 1884, p. 551 ff.
22. BOAS, F.   *Journ. R. Anth. Inst.,* xl., 1911, p. 529.
23. WISSLER, C.   *The American Indian,* New York, 1917.
24. KROEBER, A. L.   "The Languages of the American Indians," *Pop. Sci. Monthly,* lxxviii., May 1911, p. 500. (This paper has appeared since the above was in print.)

CHAPTER VII

MEXICO AND CENTRAL AMERICA

THE great Cordillera of the west runs south-east from the United States, forming several almost parallel ranges of sierra in its course through the Pacific States of Mexico, and converging again into a single range as the northern continent narrows down into the Isthmus of Panama. On comparing a relief map with one showing the distribution of nations after 1300 A.D. (1, 297), it will be seen how precisely the line of advance of the Mexicano (Aztec) was determined by the configuration of the land.

In very early times the Maya of Guatemala and Yucatan attained some degree of culture, and in the seventh century constructed the marvellous carved monuments of Guatemala. They occupied the Gulf countries, extending northwards through the present state of Vera Cruz into Tamaulipas, where the natives (Huasteka) are known to be closely akin to the present Maya. From the lowlands they spread westwards on to the plateau at least as far as the valley of Mexico, and it was they who erected the pyramid of Cholula surmounted by the temple of

G

Quetzalcoatl, their chief deity, and other monuments. They were the inventors of the system of picture-writing and of the tonalamatl almanac, which bears unmistakable signs of its origin among a tropical lowland people, for tropical animals figure largely among the twenty day-signs.

The neighbours of the Maya to the west were the Otomi, Tarasco, and the Misteca-Zapoteca family. These may not be akin to the Maya, and perhaps represent the pre-Mayan aborigines. Like the Maya, the Misteca-Zapoteca were capable of high civilisation, as witnessed by the monuments of Mitla and Monte Alban in Oajaca (1, 314).

The Maya flourished on the Mexican plateau from about 700 A.D., according to the " Anales de Quauh-titlan," until Nahoa tribes came along the Pacific coast from the north-west, and broke through between the Tarasco and Misteca. These Nahoa are linguistically related to Shoshonean tribes of the present western and south-western States of North America, some of whom still live about the Sierra Madre of north-west Mexico. It has been suggested that they are akin to tribes now existing in British Columbia, especially the Tsimshian and Nootka (5, 356, 375). According to this theory they moved down between the Rocky Mountains and the coast, attracted ever farther south. Later, other tribes occupied the greater part of the Pacific slope, thus

cutting the Nahoa off from their northern kinsfolk.
On reaching Mexico they spread as far south as Oajaca,
but never secured a foothold in this region.   They
extended in a broad belt across to the Atlantic
coast, from Vera Cruz to Coatzacoalcos, which is
still inhabited mainly by Nahoa who have overrun
or driven out other nations.   The Otomi and Tarasco
remain to the north.   In the valley by which they
came and eastwards the Nahoa encountered the
Maya, who were driven farther and farther east by
successive waves of Nahoa tribes.   Finally, a Nahoa-
speaking people, the Aztec, more powerful than their
predecessors, arrived about 1200 A.D., and some
hundred years later founded Tenochtitlan, their
lake-dwelling settlement, on the site of the present
city of Mexico.   In 1427 the Aztec formed a confederacy, which, under the leadership of Montezuma,
was destroyed by Cortez about a century afterwards.
The Aztec first came into permanent contact with,
a northern and less civilised branch of the Maya
at Tollan (modern Tula), fifty miles north of
Tenochtitlan, and called them Tolteca ("men of
Tollan"), which name came to be applied to many
elements of culture belonging to the more advanced
Maya of Guatemala and Yucatan.   Gadow (**1**, 213)
maintains that "the Mexican Empire inherited their
whole civilisation from the Toltecs, partly from those
that remained behind, partly through contact by

commerce." There were traditions that these Toltec withdrew east as far as Campeachy and Guatemala, hence the fable that their deity Quetzalcoatl, the feathered snake, disappeared into the sea, promising to return. The expelled Toltec then repaired to the territory of the kindred Maya and occupied all the best available parts of the country.

This is the view held by Förstemann (2, 540) and other authorities, but some are of opinion that the Toltec were a great and powerful nation, who, after the overthrow of their empire, migrated south, spreading their culture throughout Central America; others, again, think that they were merely a clan of the Nahoa (3, 251 ; 4, 369).

The loose application of the name Aztec to the whole of the civilisation encountered by the Spaniards on their arrival in Mexico has occasioned considerable confusion. The Aztec represent one tribe of the large Nahoa family, of which they became the military dominant stock not very long before the Spanish conquest. The name Azteca was subsequently replaced by that of Mejica, and the term Mexicano came to include all the Nahoa-speaking stock, the Mexicano dialect as that of the ruling race having superseded the rest long before the arrival of the Spaniards. Tribes outside the Nahoa group have kept the separate names given them by the Mejica, and retained by the Spaniards.

1. GADOW, H.   *Through Southern Mexico*, 1908.
2. FÖRSTEMANN, E.   *Bur. Am. Ethn.*, Bull. 28, 1904, p. 535
3. HAEBLER, K.   *The World's History* (ed. Helmolt), i., 1901, p. 180.
4. KEANE, A. H.   *Man Past and Present*, 1899.
5. PAYNE, E. J.   *History of the New World called America*, ii., 1899
6. JOYCE, T. A.   *Mexican Archæology*, 1914.
7. JOYCE, T. A.   *Central American and West Indian Archæology*,
                  1916.

CHAPTER VIII

SOUTH AMERICA

THE essential geographical features of South America are: (1) the great mountain system of the west, (2) the tropical forests of the river systems of the centre and east, (3) the vast plain of the south gradually changing in character from the rich pasturage of the Chaco to pampas and then to the bare plateaus of Patagonia.

The Cordilleras diminish in height towards the south. They are geologically speaking of recent age, and Markham suggests that at the time of the earlier civilisation they were "some two or three thousand feet lower than they are now" (1, 38), judging from the fact that mastodon bones have been discovered at a height of thirteen thousand feet in Bolivia and gigantic fossil anteaters in what is now a desert; also maize will not now ripen in the basin of Titicaca, though it must have done so in the age of the megalithic builders. These and other changes of geographical and climatic conditions must have profoundly affected the populations from time to time, but at present data are wanting for the solution of these problems.

Life in the mountain area of the west called forth that energy and resourcefulness in man which created the great Andean civilisations. The main factors in the development of Peruvian culture were the lama, the potato, and maize. Bolivia, bounded as it is on the west by the Andean civilisation, on the north and east by tropical forests, and on the south by the grass plains of the Gran Chaco, has played a part in the history of many migrations.

In accordance with the areas distinguished above the natives of South America may best be dealt with under the three following headings : i. Civilised Andeans of the Cordilleras ; ii. Backward Peoples of the forest region ; iii. Pampeans and Fuegians of the south.

i. The Andeans.—Prior to the Discovery the Inca Empire had included under its sway Aymara and other Quichua-speaking peoples. The Aymara, who should be properly called Colla, inhabited the southern province. Physically there is a close resemblance between them and the Quichua (2, ii.). The Spaniards found the Aymara occupying the area surrounding the site of the vast ruins of Tiahuanacu at the southern end of Lake Titicaca, for which some authorities consider them responsible (3, 284), but a more likely view is that of Markham (1, 47), who sees in the Aymara the descendants of the barbarian destroyers of the old megalithic culture. This civilisation is of great antiquity, dating in all probability from a period before the Cordilleras had attained their present altitude. The great population of which these ruins are evidence represents a series of movements from the south. Similar ruins are found at Cuzco, Abancay, and elsewhere, indicating the extent of the dominion of this great builder people, as to whose identity the Inca themselves were ignorant.

Survivors of these early civilisers would seem to have taken refuge at Tampu-tocco beside the deep gorge of the Apurimac, whence their descendants afterwards spread to Cuzco and founded the great Empire of the Inca about 1100 A.D., that is, some four centuries before the Spanish conquest. It is to the Inca as the dominant Quichuan people that the chief interest attaches. Their realm grew from these small beginnings till it extended from the Quito district of Ecuador to the Rio Maule in Chile, absorbing the Aymara (or Colla) in the south, and the great sea-board civilised power of Grand Chimu in the north, only to mention the most important Inca conquests (11, chap. iv).   This was the position of affairs when the Spanish Conquistadores arrived early in the sixteenth century. Small movements of peoples under the Inca may be accounted for by their system of sending loyal tribes to colonise unsettled areas and transplanting rebellious tribes to settled districts.

The Chimu population occupied the district near the modern Truxillo. They spoke a language, Mochica, which was quite distinct from Quichuan; their descendants are the Yunca now living along the coast from 5° to 10° S. lat. for whom a northward migration seems to be indicated by place-names (4, 149).

The most northerly of the great linguistic families of the Andes is that of the Chibcha-speaking peoples, Muysca, of northern Colombia. Attempts have been made to establish some relation between the Chibcha and the peoples immediately to north of the Isthmus, in which case a southward migration might be inferred. At all events when discovered, the Chibcha had long been settled in Colombia, to judge from the close connection existing between their religious conceptions and the localities which they inhabited. Although their empire was almost contiguous in the south with that of the Inca, their civilisation was quite distinct from that of the Quichua, and they retained their independence until the arrival of the Conquistadores. The Guaymi of Chiriqui, north of the Isthmus, are a surviving Chibcha people.

ii. The Backward Peoples of the forest region.— From the Cordilleras to the Atlantic and from the Rio de la Plata to the Antilles there are four great linguistic families : Tapuya, Tupi, Carib, and Arawak.

1. The Tapuya are the aborigines of eastern Brazil, the forest-dwellers of the coast-area and of the interior westwards as far as the Xingu River, a right tributary of the Amazon.   They are made up of two sections, a western branch, whom von Martius terms Gēs peoples, and an eastern branch which includes the primitive forest tribes of the east, notably the Botocudo.

The great mass of the Gēs have lived east of the Xingu since time immemorial (5, 156).   The ancient skulls discovered in the caves of Lagoa Santa present all the characteristic features of the Tapuya skull. The sambaquis or shell-mounds, however, cannot be attributed to them, as they never appear to have been navigators or fisherman, but nomadic hunters. The name by which they are known to some of their Indian neighbours is Crens ("ancients"), which points to their early occupation of the country.   Their rôle in history has been a passive one, and at the Spanish conquest their territory was practically restricted to the hill country of the interior of Brazil.   Some tribes were carried along with the great westward stream of migration.   The Semigaes, whose name and language attest their origin, penetrated to the region about the upper tributaries of the Amazon, but they have become assimilated in character to their Tupi and Carib neighbours (6, 186).

2. The original home of the Tupi lay about the

northern affluents of the La Plata. They are
essentially a water people, and in the sixteenth
century they still lived mainly by fishing and hunting, though most tribes practised agriculture to some
small extent. Their migrations have always followed
the beds of rivers or the coast. They passed down
the La Plata and on reaching the mouth turned
northwards up the coast, where they occupied a
strip of coast land, from which they drove the
tribes already in possession, calling them Tapuya
(" strangers " or " enemies "). Their migration
along the coast proceeded with comparative speed.
Arrived at the mouth of the Amazon they followed
it upwards along its southern bank, the Arawak
occupying the north bank. On the whole, the
Amazon forms a sharp division between the two,
though the existence of small detached tribes of
each race on the hostile bank proves that attempts
were made to cross the river. Tupi traditions show
that they continued to advance along the Amazon,
and it is probable that the Tupi tribes of the Xingu
and Tapajoz came down these tributaries from the
main stream (6, 191). Von den Steinen encountered
settlements of Kamayura and Auetö, Tupi tribes,
about the head-waters of the Xingu (5, 168). The
Tupi migration cannot be followed up the Amazon,
but far to the west Tupi tribes are found which have
advanced in civilisation considerably beyond the

rest of their race. These are the Omagua between
the Putumayo and the Caqueta, and the Cocama
at the confluence of the Marañon and the Ucayali.
The Omagua must have reached this region long
before the Spanish conquest, for by that time they
had learned much from the more highly civilised
peoples. The Tupi were an aggressive people
addicted to cannibalism ; those of the south called
themselves Guarani (" warriors "). The southern
Guarani about the Parana and the Uruguay were
gathered by the Jesuits into " missions " in the
early days of white influence ; a large proportion of
these Mansos (" tame ") Indians have been absorbed
by the white population.

3. The Carib have been known north of the
Amazon since the time of the Discovery. Von den
Steinen has studied Carib tribes, Bakaïri and
Nahuqua, on the Kulisehu, a head-stream of the
Xingu, and his investigations have convinced him
that von Martius and others were mistaken in sup-
posing that Carib and Tupi were descendants of a
common race, though probably there was early
intercourse between the two. He places the first
home of the Carib about the sources of the Xingu
and of the Paranatinga, a right tributary of the
Tapajoz (5, chap. xiv). Like the Tupi they are to a
great extent a fishing people, and naturally their
migrations would follow the course of rivers. On the

whole, it seems probable that they reached the mouth
of the Amazon slightly before the Tupi arrived there
by the coast route, for there is abundant evidence of
their hostile encounters with the Arawak tribes to
the north. The presence of the Tupi to the east
blocked their advance in that direction and deflected
their course northwards. Meanwhile, as we have
seen, the Tupi moved westward along the Amazon,
and southward up the Xingu and Tapajoz, thus
cutting off the migrating Carib tribes from those
remaining in their early home (6, 192).

North of the Amazon the Carib met with but a
feeble resistance from the Arawak, and they therefore spread rapidly over the northern part of the
South American continent; eventually, in the
course of centuries they prevailed from the mouth
of the Amazon to the Lagoon of Maracaibo. An
unmistakably Carib tribe is even encountered beyond
the Cordilleras in the basin of the Rio Magdalena, but
it must be regarded as an isolated group, since,
generally speaking, the civilised Andean races
effectually checked the further spread of the Carib
westwards.

Their last conquest, that of the Antilles, was
arrested by the arrival of the Spaniards. On the
large islands the population was exclusively Arawak,
but the people lived in fear of an onslaught by the
ferocious Carib, who had by this time learnt the use

of sails. On the Lesser Antilles, the Discoverers
found Carib men with Arawak wives, showing that
the islands had been conquered in that generation.
The Carib had been true to their general practice
of killing off the males and sparing the women. The
custom of eating their male foes was widespread
among the Carib tribes, and in every respect they
were fierce and much dreaded enemies, which
accounts for their rapid triumph over the less
aggressive Arawak. The southern Carib studied by
von den Steinen were found to be comparatively
harmless fishermen, so that it would seem that the
savage qualities in the race were developed in the
course of their migrations.

4. The Arawak are a very ancient typical inland
race, which points to the conclusion that their
original home must have been above the area of
periodical floods. They are to be found on the
eastern slopes of the Cordilleras from the peninsula
of Goajira to the borders of Chile, and are especially
numerous in eastern Bolivia; it may therefore be
reasonably assumed that their first home lay in
this region. This view is also supported by their
early cultivation of the tapioca-plant (manioc),
which does not grow in tropical flooded areas. At
what date they began to spread east, north-east, and
south-east it is impossible to say. It seems probable
that they encountered no earlier inhabitants in the

basins of the Amazon and Orinoco, because Arawak peoples are uniformly spread over large areas of northern South America, in fact wherever they have not been expelled by later immigrations of Tupi and Carib (6, 186). They never adopted the cannibal habits of tribes with whom they came in contact, but the Orinoco tribes became navigators and fishermen, eventually extending over the whole of the West Indies. The Arawak migration, having followed the Orinoco, proceeded through Guiana, and then some tribes turned south, crossed the Amazon, and thus reached the region about the source of the Xingu, where von den Steinen recently found settlements of their descendants (the Mehinaku, Yaulapiti, and others); the Paressi have penetrated still farther south, for there is a settlement of them north-west of Cuyaba (5, 159, 424).

iii. Pampeans and Fuegians. — This group of peoples covers the vast area south of 30° S. lat.

There is evidence to prove that in remote ages, when climatic conditions were more favourable, the pampas and the Patagonian steppe were more thickly populated than at present by Neolithic races. Implements of palæolithic type have been found in Patagonia and elsewhere; these, and human remains associated with the extinct pampas fauna (11, 237, 238), suggest great antiquity. Keane (7, i. 374) questions whether the rock inscriptions or carvings, remains of irrigation works, and stone and metal objects found on the Argentine slope of the Cordilleras and in the plains below may not possibly be ascribed to the ancestors of the megalithic builders of Tiahuanacu.

As regards the original home of the Tehuel-che (Patagonians), it appears certain that they have drifted southwards. Physically they closely resemble the Borroro, a primitive tribe living in Matto Grosso, recently studied by Ehrenreich (**8, 100, 125**) and von den Steinen (**5, 441**). The former describes their exceptional height and large round heads, in both of which respects they form a striking parallel with the tall brachycephalic Tehuel-che. If Borroro and Tehuel-che be branches of one stock, the home of their common ancestors remains to be discovered.

Beyond the southern border of the Peruvian Empire, about 35° S. lat., lived the Araucans, a compact nation which held its own against the Inca and after them the Conquistadores. Their linguistic affinities are still obscure, but physically they recall the Quichua and Aymara.

The Puel-che ("east-men"), a branch of the Araucans living on the eastern slope of the Andes, moved down the Rio Negro and came into contact with the Pampas Indians. There they have intermingled with Patagonians of the south and Guaycuru from the north, and with Europeans, giving rise to the hybrid Gaucho and others, who have been included under the term Puel-che, thus causing some confusion. More Araucan tribes, the Manzaniero, have migrated into the Argentine pampas, and these with the other Araucan peoples of the pampas have been pushed south of the Rio Negro within recent years, where they have absorbed some of the Patagonians and forced others southwards across the Rio Santa Cruz (10, 574).

Thus we have in the first place an eastward movement of Puel-che and subsequently a recoil south, as the Europeans settled about the Rio de la Plata and spread inland. To the north in Gran Chaco, a region as yet little explored, various Guaycuru-speaking tribes (Toba, Mataco, and others) remain practically in a condition of savagery. The divisions of all the Pampean tribes have been considerably modified, if not destroyed, by their nomadic mode of life, which has been brought about by the introduction of the horse.

The central and western islands of Tierra del Fuego are inhabited by Yahgan and Alakaluf, who are the true aborigines; the eastern parts are occupied by the Ona, probably a branch of the Tehuel-che, who have obviously encroached from the north (9, 7, 11).

1. MARKHAM, SIR CLEMENTS R. *The Incas of Peru*, 1910.
2. CHERVIN, A. *Anthropologie Bolivienne* (3 vols.), 1908.
3. KEANE, A. H. *The World's Peoples*, 1908.

H

4. BUCHWALD, O. VON.   Das Reich der Chimus, *Globus*, xcv., 1909.
5. STEINEN, K. VON DEN.   *Unter den Naturvölkern Zentral-Brasiliens*, 1894.
6. HAEBLER, K.   *The World's History* (ed. Helmolt), i., 1901, p. 180.
7. KEANE, A. H.   *Central and South America* (Stanford's Compend. Geog.), i., 1901.
8. EHRENREICH, P.   *Anthrop. Studien über die Urbewohner Brasiliens*, 1897.
9. HYADES, P., AND DENIKER, J.   *Mission scientifique du Cap Horn* (1882-3), 1891.
10. DENIKER, J.   *The Races of Man*, 1900.
11. JOYCE, T. A.   *South American Archæology*, 1912.
12. SCHMIDT, W.   Kulturkreise und Kulturschichten in Südamerika, *Zeits. für Ethnologie*, xlv., Berlin, 1913.

INDEX

www.ingramcontent.com/pod-product-compliance
Ingram Content Group UK Ltd.
Pitfield, Milton Keynes, MK11 3LW, UK
UKHW042146280225
455719UK00001B/148

9 781107 605862